R·E·A·L

Radical • Empathic • Acceptance • of Life

How to Live and Serve Abundantly

KHADIJAH TISHAN WASHINGTON

MSW, LCSW

This is a work of nonfiction. Some names and other identifying characteristics have been changed to protect the privacy of the individuals involved.

Library of Congress Control Number: 2020908252

ISBN 978-1-7343574-0-0

Address inquiries to: www.khadijahtishan.com

Dedication

God said let there be Zuri. He is a light that gave me what I needed and became my guide. He showed up as compassion in human form. Thank you for my radically empathic son.

Table of Contents

Introduction

Writing this book means talking about the realities, unpleasantness and disappointments associated with those who build the parts of us that make us proud and give us identity. I feel an abundance of gratitude for all the experiences and people that disappointed, harmed or shamed me.

WHO IS THIS BOOK FOR?

I still can't completely answer that question

If you have never known loss and felt unheard, this book may not be for you.

Over the last ten years as a therapist and behavioral health clinician. I noticed that many people I counseled, maybe even myself at times, had difficulty attending to the truth of their pain. Clients deal with the most difficult aspects of life until it becomes nearly unbearable to face. When they can't manage their emotions reasonably, they seek help. The process of detoxing your life begins. They get involved in strict diet plans and gym routines. They become regimented in their medication and supplements, googling all sorts of natural remedies to improve wellness. They jump in and out of relationships with the goal of affirming themselves. They gain a ton of momentum to detox and get rid of whatever it is that was hurting them. They attach themselves to anything that gives them hope that whatever they are struggling with will soon be over: an exuberant speaker or religiosity. Anything that offers an immediate sense of relief.

I don't blame them. We live in a modern world that offers almost immediate relief of symptoms with medication. We can be pain free in a matter of minutes after significant physical trauma. I wish emotional treatment could be that instantaneous!

Weeks and maybe months later, I am asking clients to do the total opposite of a detox. I am asking them to open old wounds and take a look at it. It is important that we face it, whatever "it" is, and identify how it is affecting us. Can we unpack what is really going on? It is my job to listen and encourage. I want us to unfold layer by layer, piece by piece a new kind of life. A life that is authentic and abundant. There are so many answers to our struggles. However, we must be willing and brave enough to explore. I want us to explore the beauty of the struggle.

Pain is inevitable. Suffering is optiona.

Haruki Murakam

1

Women Lie, Men Lie, Numbers Don't

There are three numbers I want you to remember. The three numbers are 22, 26, and 56.

#22– DISENCHANTMENT OF LIFE

At the age of 22, I graduated from Virginia State University with a bachelor's degree in psychology. I was single, unemployed, and pregnant. Never have I ever been so scared in my life. I was never supposed to be here. I was supposed to be different, not like my mother or grandmother. My mother had six children by the time I was born. She married a young man dealing with the trauma and effects of the Vietnam War. After many fights and a trip to the emergency room after stabbing my mother with a kitchen knife, their union was severed. Even after that ordeal, my mother had relationships and more children with two other men.

Andre was my father. When I was six years old, he died from a seizure. I noticed she never talked about him being the love of her life. There are only a handful of things I knew about him; he was my father, he loved me and my brother James, and he drank a lot. He never lived with us, and I never got the sense that my mother wanted him to live with us. Living with a man who didn't work, had seizures, and drank often along with her seven children didn't seem like a job my mother wanted to take on. My father would visit and that was it.

My grandmother had even more work. She was a single mother of ten children. My mother and her sister knew their father. My grandfather lived in the same town of Norfolk, Virginia with his wife and kids. He would come and visit often according to her. My mother described my grandfather as a doting father, even though she never knew his home phone number. He was about 30 years older than my grandmother who already had seven children when they met. My grandmother worked nights at a diner called Doumar's. I am unsure of any arrangements they had or of any assistance he provided.

I didn't want those kinds of relationships. I was going to be different. I was going to fall in love and get married. We were going to take care of our children together. According to my plan, my imaginary husband and I would take a few years to enjoy each other, explore the world, and further our careers. After I completed my Ph.D. in Psychology, we would start planning our family. I would spend the first year of our babies' lives at home nursing them and reading lots of the children's books mentioned in those online "Mocha Mom" groups. I would then work part-time while our munchkins played and gained social skills in preschool. Then my husband and I would double team them in the PTA, music and dance classes, and let's not forget coaching team sports. We were going to have a great family and life together. Celebrating every anniversary with a trip to a tropical island paradise.

See, I had a plan, and my plan should have worked. My plan would have allowed me boundless opportunities and time to choose the perfect place to grow professionally. My imaginary husband and I would buy our dream house, a four-bedroom colonial with a 2-car garage for our luxury sports SUVs. We would throw tons of parties and cookouts in our suburban neighborhood and top-rated school district. We would schedule play dates, learn Spanish together, and make homemade baby food. It was a great plan, a responsible plan, and I almost got away with it.

(20) DISENCHANTMENT OF LOVE

I FOUND HIM. . .

I was driving around downtown and DJ Boom announced that he would be at the VCU bookstore promoting a radio contest. I had been crushing on DJ Boom for some time and figured I could fake looking for grad school books while stalking my favorite DJ. I was too shy to approach him the old-fashioned way, so my plan was to browse the bookshelves and maybe give him a seductive over-the-shoulder glance with the hopes that he would notice me. Over the radio he sounded like he had a great personality, so why wouldn't he notice me?

I arrived at the bookstore, wearing tight blue jeans and a tank top. I acted quite surprised that the radio station was there. Purposely with a lot of sass in my step, I walked in front of DJ Boom while looking for grad schoolbooks. I lingered in the aisle for a while to no avail. DJ Boom didn't say a word to me. I stretched, yawned, bent over, and cleared my throat. Nothing. I even asked a salesperson where I could find the GRE prep exam book in front of DJ Boom just so he would know I was kind of smart. I did the absolute most and still nothing...

I accepted my defeat and prepared to leave. On my way out, a brown-skinned guy wearing dark tortoise shell glasses and a Power 92 t-shirt asked if I wanted to fill out an entry form for a chance to win concert tickets. I thought about it for a minute and figured if I won I would have to go to the radio station to claim my prize and DJ Boom would have one last shot with me (or the other way around). I proceeded to fill out the form.

The guy with the glasses asked if he could use my phone number to call me. Well, I hadn't even considered this turn of events. However, I was single so why not. He waited a respectable week to ask me to the movies. I was sort of nervous and wasn't completely sure I wanted to go on a date with this guy. He wasn't DJ Boom, and I didn't know what to expect. He arrived at my house, and we never made it to the movies. Instead, we ate salmon cakes and talked all night about music. You ever met someone that made you feel completely comfortable almost immediately? It was like we had always known each other all this time. Before him, I can't say any guy I dated was my friend, let alone my best friend.

I developed fast. By 5th grade, I was easily spilling out of my C cup. When my girlfriends were starting in training bras, I was overflowing in a D cup. I learned that people expected my development and sexuality to be congruent; it was easier for them. In the city, I would hear grown men make explicit comments about what they wanted to do to me. In 5th grade, I hadn't kissed a boy yet, let alone imagined some of the X-rated images described while walking down 125th street. By 7th grade, I moved upstate and in Spring Valley boys, my age preferred light-skinned Puerto Rican girls to white girls. Three years later, we moved to Chesterfield County Virginia, and a lot of boys my age preferred thin white girls. I was keenly aware that I didn't have a body like most 16-year-old girls. I knew I wasn't pretty like the Puerto Rican girls in New York. My hair wasn't long and bouncing with ringlets; it was a thick, kinky, fluffy texture. I was a sturdy size 12 and being thin and white was out of the question. My body was the preference of older men, which presented its own set of problems. Most of my experiences with men from the Harlem street corner to my mother's boyfriends could be described as just that, a problem.

Before my son's father, I was aware that men wanted something from me, and it wasn't friendship. It was a new experience to be with someone who was also friendly with me. He was always cracking jokes, and we shared an energetic sense of humor. I was from New York, and he was from Richmond. We both had to be grown-ups way too soon and had way too much responsibility. We had to take care of ourselves and others. We were the kids that never had much, so we filled up every possible moment with fun to make up for it. We had a lot in common. Our families were alike in many ways. He didn't know his father, and like me, his mother suffered from mental illness. However, my mother was higher functioning. He was a few years older than his brothers, so he did the caretaking when she could not. He was exceptionally gifted and was offered a chance to go to Open High School, which was known for their advanced placement courses and limited enrollment. He lived in low-income housing and attended a high school with the governors' children. After two semesters, he asked to be transferred back to the school with his friends. He wanted to go back to what was familiar though not necessarily better. He went back to the high school that struggled with funding and graduation rates. Later, he expressed how misguided it was that his mother let him transfer back. He had been making his own important decisions even as a child when she could not.

My mother suffered from mental illness as well. Initially, I could identify depression and anxiety. Later, I became more aware of personality disorders and informally diagnosed her. She was on Prozac for years. I remember when I was in middle school, she cried uncontrollably for days when her boyfriend Larry left. My mother put a lot of time and effort into providing for her boyfriends. Her boyfriends were always "getting on their feet," and she was always there to have what they needed. My mother was diagnosed with polio when she was 3 years old, and she would often imply that her disability made her less of a catch as compared to other women who could walk without a limp. She told me that her mother encouraged her to marry her first husband at 17 after witnessing infidelities. My grandmother told her it would be hard to find a husband as a crippled woman. My mom never seemed to question the suggestion of her mother. In her time, questioning the prophetic ideas of your parents was considered disrespectful, even if those ideas caused emotional pain. She embodied her role as less valued and compensated her insecurities with her ability to provide housing and resources to men. My mom desired to be affirmed by these men and children were a consequence of their engagement.

The brokenness that my child's father and I had in common was ultimately what tore us apart. We had similar insecurities. Neither of us trusted each other to be there and choose the other one before ourselves. We wouldn't have known what that felt like to be nurtured unconditionally in a world where we constantly had to nurture others to survive. It felt foreign to depend on someone, even each other. We needed a childhood. We needed a strong foundation and support. We needed someone to take care of us. We were the kids that had each other. We consumed each other's time. We took our minds off the heavy things that created us. Anytime we weren't doing adult things like working and classes, we were cracking jokes, laughing and just being together. It was effortless with him, and I felt safe. All the problems were behind me. It meant something to me to be his girlfriend, was needed. I was in love and felt loved.

Until that one Sunday night. It was unusual that I hadn't heard from him. My mind jumped into a shaky place. I put down my homework and called him once more. After leaving several messages, I was in my car headed to his place. His light was on, and his car was parked outside of the duplex apartment. Now I had time to imagine all the reasons he was ignoring my calls. None of them were good. My chest hurt, and my breathing was labored.

I wanted to imagine being wrong about him. I pictured myself apologizing with embarrassment. I wanted him to be okay. I wanted to trust this one. I jumped out of my car and hid in one of the bushes planted perfectly across the street so I could see his bedroom window. I tried so hard to talk myself down, "Khadijah. . .maybe he fell asleep or his phone died." I was frantically trying to piece together my story about why I was in the bushes at nearly midnight. All I could come up with was, he was my best friend.

I couldn't move. I could barely breathe. I wanted to be wrong and spend weeks apologizing for being insecure. I had two scripts in my head based on what I would see come out of his house. "I am gonna fuck you up," and, "Oh, hey is everything okay. I got worried when I didn't hear from you." Both were poised and ready to go. The longer I waited the faster my heart raced. I heard footsteps and chatter. She walked out, and I leaped inside the foyer like an Alvin Alley dancer. He had no idea I was there until he realized the door never shut. I felt fire in my throat, and I am sure my eyes were red and wet. I ran upstairs to ransack his one-bedroom apartment. I amended my script and fucked shit up instead. I grabbed some of my clothes and knocked over everything I could. There really wasn't a lot to destroy, but I tried my best. This was the beginning of heartfelt apologies and misunderstandings.

Soon after his eleven-year-old Ford Taurus stopped running, I was driving him to work near MCV hospital on my way to campus at Virginia State University. It was our life now. We commuted and ate together almost every day. We enjoyed our friends on the weekends and stayed up late all the time. I was there all the time, so I didn't have to hide in the bushes. I loved living with him and for me it was all I wanted. I was completing my undergrad in psychology, and I encouraged him to go back and finish his degree. Everything was great until it wasn't. There were a lot of highs and lows, lovemaking and disappearing acts, property damage and rebuilding. It was our cycle. I seemed to favor property damage. After an extended disappearance, he came to me and said he wanted to move in together. He lived in the expensive museum district, and his lease was up. This was probably the one time my brain cells actually registered as active. I had about a semester to graduate and didn't want to live with someone who regularly performed disappearing acts and a "brother" in need of credit repair. Shacking up was not appealing, and I wanted a real husband and family. I was in love and attached to him, but this didn't feel right. Deep down I knew living together was not going to stop the disappearing acts. I quickly declined that offer. I loved him as hard as I could, but my experiences reminded me that loving hard didn't guarantee a behavior change.

When we weren't breaking up, we had the best time together. We partied at clubs and went to shows. I still believed he needed me, and I needed him. I wasn't coming over for Sunday dinners at his grandmother's house as much, but I was still involved in some things. He sort of belonged to me when he was available to belong. In my mind, sometimes were better than no times.

It was a beautiful summer day, and he finally responded to me after an extended disappearance. He asked me to meet him at Maymont Park. He wanted to break up. I don't remember the words. He left soon after he finished talking. I sat on the bench for a long while; I couldn't move. I didn't know what we were. Sometimes we were friends — fighting — then lovers, then enemies, then friends again. All it would take was a word from him, and I was ready to love him and break more things. I couldn't resist him, and it was exhausting.

One night it almost went beyond property damage. Just a few days prior, we were visiting a grad school in Northern Virginia. We enjoyed our "on again" time just as always. Days later the shaken feeling came back, I was driving around downtown with my home-girl. At the stoplight, I glanced at the car stopped next to me, it was him and another "her." And just like that, I was in pursuit of my "off-more-than-on-again man." I could tell that my homegirl was scared, and I vaguely remember her telling me to slow down, but I couldn't hear much during those days. After a few miles, he pulled over and got out of the car to argue with me. The good time we had just a couple of days ago was a distant memory. The chasing and arguments were exhausting. I tried to break away. I was sure he didn't care about me — that much was clear from his actions. His words would say other things but what I heard inside was the loudest voice. I was caught up; letting go would hurt my heart but staying would hurt everything else.

He showed up at my graduation party and his birthday later followed. Weeks later, the smell of any kind of meat and onions made me sick. My period was late for the first time ever. Yet, I was oblivious. A lady at the daycare center where I worked in the summer before grad school noticed my food aversion and asked, "Could you be pregnant?"

I considered myself weaning from him so I stopped birth control pills, and we were only intimate one time in several months. High school sex education is absolutely right — it only takes one time. I knew the exact night we conceived; it was his birthday.

Still numb and in denial, I called and told him what this crazy lady at the daycare suggested. He was over in an hour with a pregnancy test. I couldn't muster the courage to buy a test as that was admitting guilt. He emerged from the bathroom and said, "You are pregnant!" I was in a trance-like state. I remember hearing, "Whatever you decide, I am here." I don't remember how long it took to repeat the words he told me. I had plans to go to grad school in the fall. I didn't want to become a mother like this. That last time we had sex was supposed to be the last time.

I MADE MY DECISION

After telling him I was having the baby, he abruptly met me with, "You are going to be a statistic." He said I would be another single mom and would have the baby most of the time. He had a plan to go into radio and planned to quit his full-time job. He made good on his promise. I didn't see him for months. It was my friend Katia who found me intensely crying in my bedroom consumed with fear of my unknown future. On that day, I scheduled my first therapy appointment.

He showed up sometimes, and he disappeared other times. He only came to the sonogram appointment where we found out the gender. He seemed happy to find out it was a boy. By the time I called him again, he told me to only call him when I was going into labor. He showed up for Thanksgiving and put the crib together. Some days he was friendly and excited, and others he was angry and isolated.

I was almost six months pregnant on the day of my first therapy appointment. I was in the first semester of graduate school in clinical psychology. I arrived at a spacious office with a small area with lots of toys and a sand tray for kids. I walked back to the office and sat on a large tufted chair. My therapist was a white woman that looked to be in her late 40s. He tone was even, and her affect seemed flat. I told her about how I got myself into this situation. I told her about how I cried all the time. I told her that my child's father cycled between warm to completely exasperated with me. She mostly listened and nodded. We scheduled appointments every week. After a few sessions, she told me I was depressed. She wasn't sure if I needed medication, but I needed to continue with therapy and continue to be assessed.

As time continued, I talked to her a lot about my relationship with my child's father. I told her that I couldn't depend on his support. I couldn't even depend on his presence, and when he did come around the inconsistency and lack of interest was more painful than his absence.

Therapy was helpful. It helped me to focus on a future where I wasn't sad or stressed all the time. I wasn't crying as much, and whether he was nice to me or not didn't bother me much either. Then one day at my session, my therapist made the most profound statement. I will never forget when she said, **"He will never be there for you. He is not stable, and he won't be your stability."** It was like someone told me the most authentic truth while looking me in the eye and holding my hand. It still hurt, and it wasn't what I wanted. I was quiet for a moment, and it felt like I breathed in her words. It felt like the truth; there was no compromise or negotiation. I knew then that he wasn't going to be the imaginary husband of my dreams who I shared PTA meetings with me. There wasn't going to be any more late-night talks about music and food that lasted until the sun rose the next day. He wasn't the friend I fell in love with anymore. The dream was over. I was pregnant, and now I had to figure out what life meant without my son's father. I made peace with the memory of him, but I had to focus on someone else now. Someone who needed me more than he ever could. My child needed a mother.

It's ironic how a stereotype of a single mom exists without a parallel statistic of paternal child abandonment. I am not sure if it's just difficult to measure due to the lack of birth record or if it's just easier to keep it a women's issue. This has been a complete bias. Women are to blame for single-parent households. Men have the option to leave their children. The man's choice typically creates the statistic. Teen pregnancy targets women, domestic violence prevention targets women, even programs like WIC Women, Infant, and Children. For me it was a message, WOMEN ARE RESPONSIBLE FOR CHILDREN AND MEN ARE NOT. This society continues to subscribe to this diatribe that fathering is simply an option. Outside of financial child support, the image of intact responsive fatherhood is mainly as the provider. I grew up watching sitcoms on TV about single dads. I remember Full House where a deceased wife required three grown men to take her place. Conrad from Different Stokes had Mrs. Garrett the amazing housekeeper. Men always seem to need help with the children. Women raise children while having successful careers, providing intimacy to their spouses, and maintaining a size 6 waistline and an impressive wardrobe. What if we required men to have a real voice and purpose in their families outside of financial provision? Could it happen as soon as 2020 with all we know about human development? With all the amazing single fathers, maybe we could create PIC, Parents, Infants, and Children versus WIC Women Infants and Children?

I was 22 years old, underemployed, facing single motherhood, and loss. I imagined all of life being fully available to me at 22, and I was determined not to be like them . . .my mother or grandmother. I was not going to be alone or suffering in a relationship with someone who didn't have the decency to look me in the eye when he lied to me. At 22, I had my first panic attack; my body was mimicking all the trepidation I faced. Strangled by unknown expectations, my hope and breathing were cut short. My body didn't belong to me and with the heart racing and panting, I could not control it anymore. Life shook me hard and scared the hell out of me. Now I had to share this out of control body with someone else: my baby. This was the beginning of my social work.

#26 DISENCHANTMENT OF THE FUTURE

In an effort to procure some options for myself and my child's future, I had to question that entire doctorate track. I sent out applications and had my first job interview at a local social service agency. Hey, great news! I was offered the job of a social worker with a starting salary of $26,000 a year. I had to consider the cost of childcare, getting an apartment, and my student debt repayment. Let's just be completely real and break out the calculator. At that time, I was already working part-time while in college and making almost $11 an hour. I was living at my mom's house and paying for food, a car, and insurance. I was still pretty broke. Now I was going to have a child, and I would be making an extra $1.50 per hour because $12.50 hour is $26,000 a year. And let's not forget the loans. I just didn't see how working in my psychology degree would ever get me out of poverty. I would stay broke. Working and broke. So, I made the decision to go to graduate school. I would be able to make more income and provide my child with a better lifestyle, and by all means, he would not have to grow up like I did. Broke and constantly stressed about money.

That number 26 was a real motivational number for me. At 22, I knew that making $26,000 a year would be a struggle as a single mom, so I had to find the number that would keep me comfortable. Some say the money should not matter which is ironic because money really matters. I wanted to be a superhero every Christmas and on my baby's birthdays. So, let's explore all the ways money would matter in this scenario.

If I were making \$26k a year, \$500-week, \$1000 biweekly, \$2167 monthly, \$12.50 per hour, let's break this down.

First, we have to pay income taxes, but my income would have been low enough to qualify for earned income tax credit. We won't worry about that, but we will include other governmental fees, taxes, social security tax, Medicare, and unemployment tax. These were coming out of my check every two weeks.

Estimated pre-tax and government fees
= \$2167 month - \$108 month (5%) = \$2,059

Cost of healthcare for myself and a child
= \$2,059 - \$260 month (healthcare premium deduction) = \$1799

Cost of out of pocket healthcare = varied

Cost of childcare***
= -\$350 month - (daycare program based on income) = \$1449

Car & transportation costs
= \$280 month car payment, \$250 gas, insurance, and maintenance, -\$530 = \$919

Housing rental average = \$550 month (year 2002-2004) = \$369

Electric, utilities, cable = \$150 month = \$219

Child needs* formula, diapers supplies, clothing, insurance copays \$200
= \$19

Student Loan repayment \$200 month*** = -\$181

Food, Clothing Furniture, Cellphone, Household Misc., credit cards* \$300 month = -\$481

Social and Entertainment - \$100 month = \$581

Savings=0

Retirement Savings=0

Child College Savings=0

Working with a bachelor's degree in psychology was not going to offer financial prosperity. Even if I didn't consider childcare expenses, my budget would be extremely tight, and with the expense of taking care of a child it would have been…IMPOSSIBLE!

Sitting down with an actual budget, goal sheet or even a brainstorm of my options would have been optimal at every stage of the game. But too often I became overwhelmed and simply allowed myself to float into a school or career. Or even worse, I felt limited to my situation, did nothing, remained stuck, and unhappy.

I woke up every morning thinking, "This is not what I wanted." I became depressed just ruminating about how much I didn't want to go through this and how stupid I was. This was not the life I designed in my mind nor was it the life that I wanted for my child. I was still dealing with the reality of my situation that nothing would ever be the same, and yet, I was not able to go back and get a do-over. Faced with the shock of an unplanned pregnancy, acceptance that there may not be any help or support from the father and being a product of a family already full of trauma and burden plagued my spirit. My own family never healed, so it wouldn't be able to support me. All I felt was really alone and not very smart. With all the anxiety coursing through my body and pregnancy hormones raging, I decided on graduate school. Twenty-six would not define me.

2

Debt & Emotional Debt

In 2004, when my baby boy Zuri was 2 ½ years old, I graduated from Virginia Commonwealth University with a Master of Social Work degree. This was not my original plan. I was already accepted to Virginia State University's graduate program in psychology when an amazing thing happened. I found myself 6 months pregnant and overwhelmed with life and the weight of my decisions and options. A friend found me in my bedroom sobbing. I was speechless and overcome with emotion. I just knew I was lost. I didn't have a clear plan for the future. I wasn't in love with my psychology graduate program. Not only that, but I didn't have the love, support, or affection of my child's father, and I was facing the fear of being ill-equipped as a mother.

I was given mixed messages about expectations of love by him and by my mother. His message was I will come around but not stay around. My mother's message was, "he is just a man, and his cheating and not being around is just part of the package of having a man in your life".

I had to start planning my life. How was I going to support myself and a child? I applied to Virginia Commonwealth University's MSW program and switched majors from Clinical Psychology to Clinical Social Work. I attended VCU full-time and raised my infant son. I found a nice Section 8 apartment that was income-based outside of the city. Section 8 is a federally funded rental assistance program that pays private landlords the difference between what a low-income household can afford and the fair market rent. Section 8 may refer to either the tenant-based Housing Choice Voucher (HCV) program or the Project-Based Rental Assistance (PBRA) program. In both programs, the tenant typically pays 30% of their monthly income for housing costs. ("What is Section 8?", n.d.)

I had very little income, so my rent was $97. I enrolled my son in a childcare center a few miles away from campus. The center was run by a non-profit that offered affordable childcare. I worked on weekends when my baby spent time with his father or my mother. Most of our expenses were paid by student loans. I went through periods of loving my courses, bonding with classmates, and spending sleepless nights worried about student loan debt. I learned about clinical diagnosis, social justice, and advocacy work. Over and over I heard "policy impacts practice and practice impacts policy." There were highs and lows, I also struggled with self-doubt and low self-esteem. You see, I had already messed up once, and it occurred to me that if I wasn't successful in doing this I was out of ideas and probably money. My student loans took care of my education and it also took care of us. As you could imagine, the pressure was on. Not maintaining my grades would be a swift exit out of the program. When some of my peers spent time on road trips and music concerts, I was trying to keep organized everything in my mind to stay afloat and sane.

Drop off formula at the center, complete my references for the midterm, study group on Tuesday, WIC appointment on Thursday, the baby is sick, call my internship, ask mom if she can keep Zuri late Tuesday night, I have class until 9:50 p.m. How am I going to pick him up at 10:30 p.m. and drive 35 minutes back home to Henrico, put him to bed, wake up in time to get him to the center before my 8 a.m. class?

Not to diminish my feelings, but I was beyond stressed. I couldn't even exaggerate the heavy load that I was carrying. The day my field advisor came to visit my internship at a local high school, she made the statement that I was extraordinary. I looked at her like she had snakes coming out of her forehead. She pointed out that I was doing great in most of my courses, attending a field placement, mothering an infant and working on the weekends. I hadn't even allowed myself to slow down and fully realize what I was doing. In my mind, I was one mistake away from it all falling apart. So extraordinary was not an option I gave myself.

Everything was on me, and if I didn't make it that was my fault. I had never realized that most of the people in my full-time program had no children. Some had help from parents, and some of them even had the luxury of thinking about switching majors because they changed their minds. Changing my mind was a luxury that we couldn't afford.

Although it was a lot of work and stress, I experienced some good times and met some wonderful people. I wouldn't have it any other way. This was me finding out through social work everything that I was put on earth to do. Social work and social workers had been a part of my life for as long as I could remember.

WHAT I REMEMBER. . .

I grew up in East Harlem the youngest of 7 children. My family lived in Taft housing projects, and we struggled in many ways. I had siblings that were admitted to psychiatric hospitals and some lived most of their childhood in psychiatric facilities. My mother struggled with depression, anxiety, and what I later recognized as a personality disorder. She had a series of relationships ranging from unhealthy to abusive. I remember as a child having to act as a parent to my nieces and nephews because of my sister's drug addiction and my mother's condition. We were the poster family of everything social work; transgenerational trauma, racial trauma, sexual trauma, substance abuse, domestic violence, poverty, fatherlessness, mental illness, parentified children, unforgiveness, incarceration, foster care system, secrets. . . a lot of family secrets. EVERYTHING!

Some of us were touched, many were hurt. The people who hurt us were our family, and some were friends of the family. No one ever felt secure in their place in this family. Others left and some were taken away. We were all children who never got a chance to fully enjoy our childhood. We had to find a way to survive and live, which meant growing up faster than our stated age. We struggled to hold on to each other and still struggle to hold on to each other.

I admired people who wanted to learn more about people because I wanted to learn more about "us." I admired the sophisticated vernacular of Frasier Crane on the TV show Cheers. I knew I wanted to be like that. I wanted to be like Freud. I wanted to know how a family like mine came to be a family like mine. Armed with a bachelor's in psychology and a Master of Social Work, I came closer to finding my answer and myself.

3

#56

What does this have to do with #56?

Fifty-six thousand dollars was the total of my student loans for all my education and living expenses. After all the hard work and struggles, I was graduating with $56,000 of debt before I received my first paycheck. My first position after grad school was a job working in child protective services and foster care. My salary was $26,500. Yes, there it is again; dang it, 26. The number 26 will not define me!

WE DON'T DO IT FOR THE MONEY? OR DO WE?

My Answer: Maslow's Hierarchy of Needs Theory proposes that human motivation begins with meeting physiological needs and continues to self-actualization. Although some of today's scholars believe these levels are continuous and overlapping. It is extremely difficult to undergo major psychological shifts when you are hungry or homeless. Money and resources are basic needs without which we can go no further. Social work continues to be a profession linked with charity work, poverty, and 'tree-hugging'. I have never heard a social worker ever talk about 'dominating the field', 'incentives', 'profits', 'scaling' or 'branding.' That's simply not social work jargon, and in my 15 years of social work, I had no understanding of the social, financial, and political impact of my own work. I haven't attended a course or continuing education workshops on the "economics" of my work.

There is a philosophical disconnect. Perhaps, a belief that contemplating compensation and assessing value to the community means that you are not truly committed to the community. I wanted to make a difference in the world, but no one told me how to take care of myself. Before I could address the weight of the world I was weighed down with debt. I was raised in debt; no one explained how to stay out of it. I was in a home where my mother filed bankruptcy and avoided friends she borrowed money from who wanted to be paid back. We moved all the time to avoid household bills. There weren't any new nice things because there was always something to pay for. I wanted to get so much from life but I owed so much just to live. Just thinking about $56,000 feels insurmountable, especially when you have nothing. The challenge of having an honorable profession and wanting to honor its work and study with earnings in proportion to the value to society is not often embraced.

Growing up in poverty created a sense of "figure it out" because money, that was so needed, was not available. It also created a great amount of anxiety. I didn't understand how to manage money or even make more of it.

I had no concept of business, profit, loss or passive income. All I remember is the harshness of poverty. We moved every year from 6th to 11th grade. Asking my mother for clothing was uncomfortable. The nicer the neighborhood we moved into the better the kids dressed. I knew I couldn't ask for Guess jeans and Nike sneakers like the other teenagers. I wore the kind of clothes that frayed easily, were poorly constructed, and didn't have designer labels. I couldn't get my hair styled every couple of weeks, so I learned how to braid my own hair at home and reused the extensions in my hair throughout the year for an updated look. Part of my embarrassment was solved because soon I would be moving, and my classmates wouldn't know I didn't have a wardrobe of clothes to wear. Starting over every year through my teen years with money insecurity, disconnected friendships, poor body image, and low self-esteem was overwhelming. Being poor was stressful as a child and as an adult. Even as a child, I remember knots in my stomach because I hated asking for money. I would again be reminded, "We didn't have money." The idea of poverty did nothing for my self-esteem. Even worse, I came to fear and resist money. It was in my 30's that I was opened to the possibility of a plan to cover expenses and savings. It took that many years to recover and create a new relationship with money. The mindset shift occurred when I became curious about being rich. I had to think outside of the box — past wages and working. I had to go a bit deeper into my animosity toward money as well as acknowledge the savior it had provided. The mindset shift, coupled with technological resources and creativity created a new world for me and a relationship with work and income.

Most social workers are not familiar with bookkeeping. We have no idea of the short and long-term financial impact of our work. My hope is once these conversations happen regularly, we will truly begin to value our place and need in society. Unfortunately, if we fail to look at the money people will not see the value. If we aren't financially literate, we won't understand the full impact of how our quality of life as a social worker impacts the quality of work and services that we provide to people who need all that we have to give. My professional goals and pursuits changed when I no longer had to worry about money. When I was broke, I was not able to do my best work or most creative work. It wasn't the work I loved to do. I just got a paycheck. Sometimes, I didn't work. I often showed up because of my fear of starvation and need to pay a car note. I was not effective or committed. My entire spirit was consumed with worry. My thoughts and creativity were locked up. Do we see what we are risking by not talking about money — by ignoring it? By focusing on some kind of abstract "greater good" that does not seem to consider you nor your needs, your family nor your prosperity, burnout will arrive. There are social workers employed today who cannot afford to live in the city that they serve. There are social workers who are one paycheck away from being a client in need of social services. Too many of us are living frighteningly close to the edge of poverty. Let's change the narrative of simply "doing good" to "adding value" to the world.

Our work is far too important for any of us not to enjoy living full lives of prosperity.

WHY NOT JUST BE A LIFE COACH IT'S LIKE THE SAME THING

During the last decade, the media has introduced a variety of colorful personalities who have entered the lives of people struggling with everything from weight loss to recovery. This idea of "life coaching" became huge. Often, highly complex trauma and addictions were being addressed in 52 edited television minutes. Even I had to wonder, why am I not life coaching? It had to be more lucrative than $26,000 per year. It seemed "self-help" blossomed into talk shows and social media followers. Let's be clear; some programming and content are very socially responsible about offering resources and long-term care available with mental health professionals. But, some will never truly appreciate the difficulty and commitment needed to address mental health as a holistic support system that is accessible for recovery.

The life coaching industry is one of the largest and fastest-growing industries. According to projections by the Bureau of Labor Studies, the consulting services industry is responsible for most of the employment growth in professional and business services. Life coaches help people identify and pursue goals in some of the same ways that clinicians do. However, a clinical social worker is equipped with a wealth of knowledge and supervised experience to apply theoretic models and perspectives on human behavior. Life coaches may tap into diverse motivational and philosophical belief systems to assist individuals in manifesting their goals. Long story short, two different roles.

But, if you look at the fame and financial compensation of well-known life coaches, there might be a bit of temptation to switch occupations. I think the average person would struggle to name practicing clinicians who have made professional contributions in mental health. I recently watched an episode of Iyanla fixing the life of someone. It opens with a heart-wrenching story of a life with drug addiction, abuse, molestation, abandonment to now a life desperately spiraling down. At 22 minutes into the show, there is a confrontation of desperate lives. After screaming, cussing and defensive pleas, the show reveals a new found hope in 45 minutes. We are left with all the emotional turmoil, wondering whether to love them or hate them. I have a difficult time convincing people to commit to therapy, possibly for months, when so many people place hope in the false reality of reality tv.

These highly dramatized 45 minute televised interventions, interrupted by sponsored marketing messages, elevated life coaches to celebrities. More people recognize Iyanla Vanzant or Dr. Phil before their local licensed mental health professionals. Some coaches are incredibly insightful and really support people in areas that help them grow in personal relationships, health, and business. They provide an incredibly valuable service. Along with their work, the media offers them endorsements, fame, and money . . . a lot of money.

So why can't the therapist next door follow that same model to financial prosperity? We've practiced years of effective communication. We often hear what is said and listen to what is not. We have learned the skills to assess nonverbal communication and track behaviors that offer some insight into the source of an issue. We spend time and money obtaining courses for continuing education hours each year to sharpen our skills and enhance our practice. We practice an interdisciplinary profession that seeks to facilitate the welfare of communities, individuals, and societies. We facilitate social change, development, cohesion, and empowerment not to mention psychotherapy. So, how do we monetize that value and become a worldwide brand?

RICH AND FAMOUS SOCIAL WORKERS

You do what Brene Brown did! Brene spent 16 years studying vulnerability, courage, shame, and empathy. She has aligned herself with Oprah annnnnnnd. hello. cha-ching!

Pointless side note: In my mind, Oprah is my mom and Les Brown is my dad. Anyway, back to work.

Brene's work taps into the human connection and has touched the hearts of thousands of people with her work. I can't think of anything more noble. I am sure she was committed to her work and what she wanted to offer to the world. When she took her knowledge, skills, and passion and scaled it to impact masses, she prospered.

Please note I will never tell my kid, "Do what you love and don't worry about the money." When I was broke, money was all I could think about. As with most broke people, the thoughts around money are exhausting. So instead, *I tell him 'Do what loves you'! You have amazing talents and abilities, and you must figure out how to use that to create the life that you desire. Find an amazing way to serve.*

In a profession where the statement, "If you're in it for the money you are in the wrong profession" is our battle cry. Brene has an estimated net worth of nearly 3 million dollars and 30 million views on her Ted Talk, "The Power of Vulnerability."

Brene didn't invent any new emotions. She simply studied what was already there and clearly committed to her work. She commands an average of $25,000 per speaking engagement. Writing and talking to people about the things we deeply care about. So many of us are already halfway there. Brene moved her passion from the university lecture halls to our living rooms in the form of media. Are you furiously committed to your work? If so, this is a great opportunity to grow. If not, this is a great opportunity to leave and find the work that loves you! What if social workers were armed with the knowledge of how to deliver and package their unique brand of service and offered those skills to companies, groups, and individuals. What if all it takes is, not a shift to life coaching but a complete mind shift in social work.

Now let's talk about the amazing motivational speaker and six-time best-selling author Lisa Nichols. Before you jump down my throat and say she is not a "social worker," allow me to share a bit of her past. Lisa tells the incredible story of being a single mother unable to buy diapers for her son because she only had $12 in her bank account (sounds familiar). She describes this as starting from rock bottom. During her "rock bottom" experience, Lisa found a job running the Family Resource Center for the Los Angeles Unified School District. She began saving towards her dream that was not fully evolved. She then started a program called "Motivating the Teen Spirit" where she worked to empower teens by helping them make choices based on integrity. Now, please tell me how this is not social work. It sounds like social work, smells like social work, and yes, feels a lot like social work. People in our field are changing lives every day.

Lisa's impact became greater as she developed her passion for motivating people, she became a great speaker, writer, and businesswoman. Nichols eventually founded Motivating the Masses, a massive training resource for personal and professional development that went public. She was also featured in the best-selling book *The Secret*.

Just FYI, there is an entire therapeutic intervention called motivational interviewing (MIT). MIT is a directive client-centered counseling technique where the counselor facilitates changes with the use of their relationship with a client. MIT was developed by clinical psychologists William R. Miller and Stephen Rollnick.

Many more people have heard of Lisa Nichols versus Miller & Rollnick. Lisa is more than research or testing. She is a person who has an amazing underdog story and has climbed insurmountable odds to grow herself and her business. We can reach out and touch Lisa's story. Even as we utilize the tools of motivation, the art of how we create and deliver services is so different. In grad school, someone told me, "Social work is a science and an art. The science is the research but how you use the research and intervention is the art.

I Don't Just Take Kids Away!

It's a profession that provides value to the lives of so many. Social work produces billions of dollars in the industry. So, we must always define our role and value to the world. In short, I am more than a do-gooder. I don't want to take your kids, and I am not collecting for the needy. The need to redefine means creating more wealth and abundance in order to influence more change in the world. If money were not a consideration, what would you be doing right now?

Okay after the tropical vacation, what would you be doing in the world?

We have explored the financial and social value of our work; now, we must begin to redefine our brand. For the most part, colleges and universities teach us how to be a professional social worker. We adhere to a code of ethics and state licensure regulations, and we must realize the necessity of education in ways to create industry. We all know that prosperity and quality of life are connected. Poverty increases adverse health outcomes, low graduation rate, and increased rates of victimization.

Deconstructing Our Role

I've had some wonderful and exciting experiences to make way for my current role. I work for a great healthcare company that allows me flexibility creativity, and time to learn and train in new skill sets and technology. It wasn't always this way though. There are far more businesses that do not support their social workers. I believe a huge barrier to social workers' professional development is the lack of commitment to self-care for employees. Employers must realize self-care is an asset in building a successful business. Check out the most recent statistic on the cost of sick days.

I have faced personal and ethical dilemmas. Soon after becoming licensed as a social worker in a public nonprofit agency, I was offered a job in a private agency. I was elated to be earning $10,000 more annually, and as we revealed earlier, I was thoroughly broke and was raised mostly in poverty and financial instability. I knew then that "broke life" wasn't for me. I had received extensive training in child and family mental health and was excited to finally make some "real money." I worked at a small startup community mental health agency. Although my position was essential to this agency remaining in compliance with the licensing board, I was not the boss. In simpler terms, they needed me to provide clinical oversight to operate this business, but I was not an owner and my clinical guidance was equated to "optional suggestions" for this agency. I worked for three men who had no background in social work, mental health or even the community that they were serving. My role was to ensure this company provided the best mental health services to children and families, and their objective was profit. You can already imagine how this ended. When agency owners look at your work solely from an investor's perspective, and you adhere to clinical integrity, there will be problems. Not only the clash of philosophical differences but also ethical dilemmas. I learned my male counterpart that actually had less experience and less responsibility earned nearly $40,000 more than me. **YES, I SAID $40,000 more than me!!!** Sexism is alive and well even in social work.

I left that agency due to the ethical conflict. Unfortunately, the move created another situation of desperation and stress to find another position. Often, that is the way our industry is set up. When we do the right thing, we can find ourselves out of a job or in hostile work environments. We may essentially be employed by people who haven't any love or understanding of our work. Your employers may not be committed to your ethical, professional or personal growth.

Unfortunately, everyone is not financially able to leave a higher paying position. I left this unethical agency for another position that paid the same. This position required a ridiculously intense schedule. I found myself working more than 50 hours a week. I also accumulated unpaid hours to this job during my venting sessions with my best friends on the drive home.

I ask that you give me permission to paint a picture of a day in this situation

Unethical Agency LLC offered the flexibility to work from home some days. I created my schedule and supervised 6-8 counselors. I was able to create a parent engagement program and work in the community. I took days off for vacation and family time without issue.

Ethical Agency LLC offered the same salary. I managed school-based and after school programs for children. I was the clinical supervisor for all the counselors in five schools (about 10 counselors). I supervised all the counselors and support staff in the afterschool program and two licensed-eligible clinicians. I was also part of the management team and the clinical team. My responsibilities included the review of all clinical notes with a two-day turnaround time as well as being in attendance for Individual Education Plan (IEP) meetings and Communities in School meetings. managed referrals, assessments, and clinical training of the teams in two regions. Days off weren't in sight unless schools were closed. Many times, the closing of school didn't give me a break because of the training that needed to be completed.

My personal life and health suffered greatly. I found myself having almost constant panic attacks, being sick more than I was well, and generally lying in bed speechless, tearful, and afraid during much of my time off. I can't recall how many times I was able to come home and make dinner, go for a walk or watch a movie with my family. The weekend was simply the time I got to lay in bed and attempt to recover. I was in my second job that same year, and I didn't want another job on my resume so soon. I later learned that my position was open because the clinician I replaced was involved in a fatal car accident on her way back to work from a lunch break. I began to envision myself driving back and forth between schools and meetings, being tired much of the day. I was rushing back to work, as I assumed, she was doing that day and so many other days. I couldn't envision myself living this way. Fortunately, I had options by that time. After reflecting on my situation, I chose me. I made the decision to resign and take some time off.

The Cost of Social Working; Life or Death

During this season, I was facing major health and quality of life issues. Someone viewing my resume and judging my ability to be responsible caused great worry and anxiety

Here are some words of advice: *When considering your health and the opinions of others, always choose to focus on your health.* This season caused me to reflect on my funeral and what others would say or think of me during this event. Yes, I said funeral. Almost seven months after resigning to take care of me, I decided to start my own private practice. Just prior to my opening, it was discovered by accident and divine intervention that I had a rare tumor called a pheochromocytoma on my right adrenal gland. I was so focused on my career climb and obtaining some hope of financial stability that I just kept working and going to my doctor complaining about my symptoms. I was misdiagnosed as simply being overworked, underpaid, and overwhelmed. Because I was so focused on the stress and desperation of work, I never considered visiting another doctor for a second opinion. If I would have continued on that path, I would have died of a hypertensive stroke. No one should ever have to choose between work and their own life.

The Story of my Accidental Divine Intervention

Ironically my condition was discovered when I was hanging out with my son and eating hot wings. I ate one of his wings and started feeling a lot of pressure in my chest like bad heartburn. Then, it got worse. I was taken to the ER in severe pain and skyrocketing blood pressure. I was scared, but more than scared. . .I was terrified. The doctors diagnosed me with a bad gallbladder, but during the ultrasound of my gallbladder, they found a five-centimeter tumor on my right adrenal gland. In all fairness, the job did not create the tumor, but how many of us know of someone who has health challenges that they are not actively addressing because of their "have to"? They have to go to work, have to pick up the kids, have to work an extra job.

We need to make a living and contribute to our families. But, if those jobs do not support our wellness and professional development, then we must prioritize ourselves. We have to connect to people in our field and outside of this field to increase innovation, shared values and wellness. Not only should we prescribe self-care, but we should also serve as a leading example. I won't say all social workers or social service agencies support a workplace of self-care and ethical values. In fact, I know many more stories about the places that do not. However, if I had a standard of personal self-care, I would have known to listen to my body first. I cannot do any of this amazing work if I am not alive.

4

The Path You Chose and the Path that's Chosen

Cheers!!!

My earliest impression of a helping professional was watching the television sitcom Cheers when I was 11 years old. The character Frazier Crane was a British psychologist that spent his evenings in a bar named Cheers. I recall loving his accent and his use of vocabulary. I gathered that psychologists spoke very sophisticated words in a room with a sofa and made people feel better. I have an entirely different observation today. In the 80s, an 11-year-old black girl, born and raised in the projects of Harlem New York, envisioning herself as a psychologist, was a rarity. The incredible imagination of children explains my love of working with them. Their imagination hasn't been structured into "boxes" of what the world says is "realistic". They imagine themselves as queens, mothers, heck, even a tiger. Nothing is impossible for a child until the world tells them "no", "stop", or "be careful." It's a beautiful thing to witness a child telling the world, "This is who I am," instead of the world telling the child, "This is who you are."

THE PATH YOU CHOSE AND THE PATH THAT'S CHOSEN

I imagined being a psychologist like Dr. Frasier Crane. As the youngest of seven with a mom who was often stressed out and working through some complicated emotions, most things were not options. They were mandatory. By the time I was about ten, I had the opportunity to leave New York City with my family to visit Disney World in Orlando, FL and the opportunity to visit Washington, D.C. It may not have seemed like a lot to others, but this was a big deal to me at the time because some kids never left the neighborhood. When I was seven years old, my mother signed me up for the Fresh Air Fund, a camp where city kids spend two weeks with a family in the suburbs of upstate New York. The Fresh Air Fund has provided free summer experiences to more than 1.8 million New York City children from low income communities since 1877. Each summer, thousands of children visit volunteer host families in rural and suburban communities along the East Coast and Southern Canada or attend six Fresh Air camps in upstate New York. Young people also participate in year-round leadership and educational programs. The Fresh Air Fund is an independent not-for-profit agency *("The Fresh Air Fund fact sheet 2019", n.d.)*.

The first family I visited was French Canadian and didn't speak very much English, but at seven years old, I could freely jibber-jabber in any language, so I didn't mind. I simply matched their jibber-jabber with my jibber-jabber, and we were talking! Up until that time, the only cultural exposure I had was with the Puerto Ricans and Dominicans in my neighborhood. My time with this family was spent mostly in their garden outside in the sun. This was the first time I saw food growing out of the ground.

The Fresh Air Fund matched me with a different family the following summer. The Scannells lived in a small town near Rochester NY. The family called my home the night before my trip to introduce themselves. They told me their names: Nancy, Jim, Jessica, and Jocelyn. Jocelyn was the younger sister and would be there when they picked me up. Jessica was away volunteering with children in New York City. Later, Jessica would spend time in India. They asked my mom about my favorite foods. She told them I loved hotdogs. I tried to correct her while she was on the phone, and she shewed me away. My favorite food was pizza. My brother was the one who liked hotdogs. My mom never asked me about my favorite food, so I guess I understood why she didn't know. The next day I arrived on a bus filled with excited New York City kids eager to meet their new suburban families. I felt anxious while gathering my belongings. I would live with the Scannells for two weeks. Thoughts swirled through my mind. *What if they don't like me? What if their food tastes nasty?* I looked for the two people who described themselves over the phone. I looked around for a "white mom" with dark brown hair and a daughter with blonde hair. A lot of women matched that description. I continued to search for my summer family to no avail. Finally, a camp counselor introduced me to my new family.

The summer was full of new experiences. I spent the summer with the Scannells chasing cats, feeding dogs, and going to baseball games. I got to be a carefree kid who only did one chore on the weekends. I watched their daughter play a lot of soccer games. Sometimes we took a drive into town to get chocolate dipped ice cream cones after dinner. While this was my first summer with this family, it would not be my last. Each summer with the Scannells we took a trip — several times to Lake Canandaigua but also to Boston and Canada.

After several summers with the Scannell family, I openly referred to them as my "white family." Visiting the Scannells created an awareness that people had more options in life other than what I was familiar with or exposed to in my lifetime. Many of those options were connected to race and money. Everyone seemed to have a Volvo or Jeep and lived in really big houses. I didn't meet anyone who didn't have a father at home. The fathers didn't work for the Departments of Sanitation or Transit as they did where I was from. Instead, the fathers worked at banks or universities. Sometimes I didn't understand what kind of work they did, but I knew they had money.

I loved summers with the Scannells. They would always ask me about what I was reading and what I liked. I was able to order anything I wanted. They made sure all the children read books every day. I mostly read Judy Bloom. The Scannells were always attentive and complimenting me about my reading and comprehension. My mother never asked me to read, but she did give us money for good grades. Like Dr. Frazier Crane, I was observant and noticed just how differently we lived. The first place the Scannells and I visited together was the supermarket for some treats. I arrived and walked through the aisles, then yelled out, "Where are all the Black people?" I don't recall an answer just the uncomfortable look on their faces. It had not occurred to me that there were places that Black people did not live. Experiencing the "white world," I was somewhat shocked that no one seemed to notice the Black people who were missing. I was less shocked to notice that Black people in Harlem never mentioned the lack of White people. One day the mom, Nancy, tried to explain to me why I didn't need to refer to them as my "white" family. She said, "When we look at you, we don't see color." I didn't understand that because I saw myself as Black, and being with them, I was never able to un-see it. Our lives seemed so different that color became the way I could define the differences. They lived in a big house with a couple of dogs, lots of cats, rabbits, and a horse named Winston. I never knew a horse could be a pet. Nancy stayed at home and tended to the house and children. Everything was white.

In my world, no one ever bothered to ask me anything. It was of no concern or consequence what I thought or desired. In my world, all the mothers worked. They wore jackets, skirts with pantyhose and sneakers, and they were always walking fast to catch the Number 2 or 4 bus downtown. Some of the mothers had a husband but most did not. I only ever met a few of my friends' fathers and that was when they were being picked up on weekends. I knew better than to ask my mother for anything other than a happy meal from the McDonald's menu. Sometimes I would get fancy and request extra pickles. If we got Chinese carryout, I shared it with my brother and niece. It was always the same order, chicken wings and pork fried rice.

It didn't take long for me to figure out that the Scannells were rich. I went with mom Nancy to run some errands. On the way to the store, she stopped at the ATM and withdrew $300. I counted it quickly in silence. I had never seen that much cash, and anyone who had $300 at one time was definitely rich to me. In my world, I dreaded the embarrassment of having to go to the store with the food stamps my mother gave us. I would have loved to take a card to get cash out for food. Every time I went to C- Town supermarket with food stamps in my pocket, I was on a mission to leave unseen. I anxiously moved throughout the store, quickly grabbing items from my mother's list and putting them in my cart. I then lapped the store once more to ensure that none of my friends were shopping. I didn't want them to come behind me in the checkout line and see that I was paying with food stamps. Once the store was clear of any familiar faces, I chose the empty check-out line and hurried to bag up the groceries. Even though I lived in a low-income housing development like some of my friends, there was a special kind of shame that came with using food stamps. After seeing Nancy pulling out a cool $300, traveling out of state and country borders having prepared meals every night, and giving me my own room, I knew then "being rich" was something I would strive to be in the future. I remember every year that went by I looked forward to summers with my "white family." One summer I didn't want to leave I was about 11 and I wanted to stay and feed the animals. I wanted to ride Winston even if I was too afraid to stay on the saddle. It was so calm living there. There was no yelling, fighting or rushing you out of the bathroom. I wanted to go to private school and play soccer. I had never played before, but I imagined I would have been good at it. The Scannells tried to explain to me that my mom and siblings would miss me too much. I didn't believe them. I had to go back on the bus full of city kids loaded up with all the clothes and toys their Fresh Air families gave them. It was loud, and I was quiet. We arrived at the Port Authority Bus Terminal, and we were gathered into a designated area while we waited for our parents to pick us up. Most of the kids were gone in 30 minutes, and I was still there. The counselor asked me for my home number again. I waited for at least another hour. A counselor thought I was sad because my mom forgot about me and tried to distract me with a game. She was wrong. I was sad because I had just left the people who never would have forgotten to pick me up. My older sister Darlene came to pick me up a while later. She said something about mommy just calling her. I didn't listen, and I didn't care. When I arrived home, my siblings asked me what I got. I dropped my bags and ran to the bathroom. My face was hot and wet, and the apartment felt a lot smaller and louder than I remembered. My mom asked, *"What's wrong?"* I replied, *"I don't want to be here."*

This was when I chose the family that I wanted. At 11, I decided I wanted a husband who lived with us and had an important job. I wanted to stay at home and take care of the children and drive a Volvo. We were going to cook and eat well every night. I wanted to be rich and get money from the ATM whenever I wanted. I would choose not to argue about money and always ask my kids a lot of questions about themselves and their feelings. As a mom, I would make sure my kids were reading and I would let them order from any side of the menu. That day I chose the family that I wanted.

I remained in a state of frustration and exhaustion for the remainder of the summer. I was over the chaos in my family and over all the people in the apartment. Once I knew my chosen family was out there, I didn't have the time or energy to argue with my brother about popsicles or having to go play with the kids behind the building. These people didn't know anything about me because they never bothered to ask. I knew that my "white family" didn't really like it when I called them "white" or "rich." But, it was the opposite for me, I would have loved to be white and rich. I practiced being white all the time just in case they decided that I could stay with them. I wrapped that white towel around my head and got to swinging my imaginary hair in front of the bathroom mirror. I would not experience another Easter Sunday ear burn from the hot comb. I would love to have seen my father go out and work and give money to my mom. I would have loved being driven around in the Volvo afterschool. Everyone spoke differently to each other and I practiced that too. White people seemed concerned about my happiness. I saw that family was important to them. One summer, Mr Scannell took me to a park in Boston named after his grandfather. I had no idea what kind of impact someone had to have on a community to have a park named after them, but I knew it was important. So, yes I will take it make me white!!! The Fresh Air Fund and the Scannell family shaped my ideals around family and created a path for me to begin to question what believed I wanted in my life. I am so thankful for that early exposure which set into motion all I questioned in my family of origin. Today, I question the cultural trauma of the past and impact on how we came to know each other and treated each other. I question how my family would have been different if afforded opportunities and resources.

Today, I love being in my beautiful brown skin after years of unpacking those pieces of my identity. Kindness, love, and connection are not assigned to a race. However, there are all sorts of challenges along the way when you think about the trauma of history. How difficult is it to focus on love when you are obsessed with survival? I would imagine it is as difficult as making rational decisions when you are being suffocated. The Scannell family was given the privilege to focus on love and family because their human rights were respected. They were able to have a big home and animals because their human rights were respected. My story is like so many brown skinned girls. We had to fight for our path. We had to struggle.

I appreciate my beauty even more because I realize that I had to find it. I had to seek and find myself. I had to question all the noise and societal statistics that informed my thinking and thus my behavior. I struggled to find compassion and knowledge of myself.

THE PATH OF CHAOS AND CONFUSION

I discovered that social workers were involved with my family in one way or another for most of my life. I was the youngest of 7 children born to a single mom in East Harlem, New York. My mother moved from Norfolk, Virginia as a teen, and she was the youngest of 10 children in a single-parent household.

WE WERE NOTHING LIKE THE SCANNELLS

My early memories are erratic. I remember living in a tenement building at 218 West 112th Street. I loved going down to Mr. Tall's candy shop on the corner for penny candy. I loved dressing up for Halloween and going trick-

or-treating. I knew most people on my block, and they knew us. Some would come over from time to time and babysit us. We lived with my mom and grandmother in a 2-bedroom apartment on the 7th floor. All the kids slept in the living room, and my mother and grandmother had their own room. I remember our apartment having mice, which led to my intense fear of them. Back then, my mom attended Fordham University. I later referred to Jimmy Carter as the best President when she told me she went to school for free. Jimmy Carter established the Department of Education and programs to make education more accessible to the less advantaged. My mother graduated college and began working for the city of New York. We moved to Taft Housing Projects, which was located about 4 blocks away on East 112th Street.

I attended East Calvary Day Care, then the preschool across the street. My sister was responsible for walking me across the street to school. She would make me angry because she often woke up late, which meant I would not get to school on time. I loved school, and if I got there too late, I would miss graham crackers and milk, and my life would be incomplete for the remainder of the day.

My father, Andre, didn't live with us. He lived with his mother, my Grandma Campbell. I remember him visiting and picking me up and holding me. I do not remember much else. Before he died, I remember him having seizures in bed when I laid next to him. The only detail I know about his death was that he died alone without someone there to help him. Later, I found out that he drank and drinking made his seizures worse and more frequent. I was told he developed seizures after being severely beaten by a police officer when he attempted to jump a train turnstile without paying. I wore a pink dress with pleated chiffon to his funeral. Afterward, I left with my Grandma Campbell and rode through Brooklyn in her station wagon. After my father died, Grandma Campbell would come to pick me up some weekends and take me to Brooklyn. She cooked for me, and one day she introduced me to Grandpa Campbell. I only remember meeting him once. Sundays she ushered all day and night in the church. After lunch, I would allow the vibrations of the clapping and the bass to rock me off to sleep in the pew.

My Empty Path

I soon realized I didn't know what happened to many of my siblings. Social workers were there from the start. I wasn't born by the time Darlene left. She was the second born and went to the psychiatric hospital when she was nine. She was shuttled through psychiatric facilities and group homes until she was a legal adult. No one ever told me where she lived when I was a kid, and I never visited her. Later, my mother told me Darlene went away because she was hiding knives under her pillow with a plan to stab my mom. My only childhood memories of her are from the sepia-toned pictures taken of her in our photo album. In one picture, she was lined up in front of our building with the rest of our siblings wearing a pastel-colored dress on Easter Sunday. I don't remember any Christmases or Thanksgivings with Darlene, not even when she was an adult. When I was about five years old, we moved to Taft Projects. Darlene never moved in, but when she had a baby at 14, the baby lived with us. I was only two years older than baby Eva, and I always remember her being there. I met Darlene when she was grown, and she came back to get her daughter. They didn't live together long; I heard something about her spanking Eva too much. Eva never came back. She went to live with a lady in Queens.

Darlene wasn't the only one who left. Damon left for the psychiatric hospital when he was 8 a few years later. He was the 5th born child, and the first son after four daughters. In our photo album, I saw his baby pictures.

He had cornrows in his hair, smiling in the park. I remember a few Christmases together, but by the time I started first grade, Damon was gone. He was away for a long time. One Saturday morning, we woke up early and looked for our "good clothes." My hair was brushed in ponytails, and we waited downstairs for a car to pick us up to go see Damon. I looked out the back window and saw seagulls flying above the river. We arrived at what looked like a campground. We ran around with soccer balls and raced each other barefoot in the grass. The city seemed far away. We were across the river and in the quiet of land and trees. We played all day; our clothes damp with sweat and smell of the outdoors. At sunset, we were prompted to gather and get ready to go. I wondered why Damon got to stay at summer camp. We left him behind, and I fell asleep on the way home. At that age, I didn't understand, so I was envious, I thought to myself, "Why does Damon get to stay at camp all year, and I only get to go in the summer?" He left as an 8-year-old boy and returned as a 16-year-old teenager. Later, my mom told me Damon had to leave because he was seeing and hearing things that weren't there. My aunt told me someone hurt him when he was a little boy, but she never told me who or how they hurt him. Damon returned as a petulant teenager ready to make up for all the time he had lost while away at "camp." The time was brief. Soon he was sent up to Riker's Island jail; he was accused of stealing a wallet along with some other boys from another neighborhood. He was gone again.

Traveling to see Damon at Riker's was much longer than the visit ever was. I was 12 when my sister Lonnie and I took several buses up to see him there. There were a lot of kids waiting in the room, and couples were doing their best to touch, kiss or embrace around the table that separated them. Their touch seemed so intense — not passionate but more desperate. Their precious time ticked away. I saw grown men in jumpers, and my brother was 16 and still looked like a boy. Damon had basically been locked up most of his life. Now, he was with grown men. This didn't look like a camp. There were no places to run around or play kickball. This was hard. The walls, the chairs, and the emotions hard and desperate like the couples visiting. There were no wide-open spaces of grass and trees. The space felt drained of any color, dingy, and gray. There was no hue present that might evoke an emotion of warmth or peace. The air was stale, heavy, and filled with musty body odors melding with soiled diapers. We heard the loud whispers and the excitement of lovers who had not seen each other in so many weeks or months. There were toys laying around and a lot of kids. He was a child, and we left him there again.

LOSING LONNIE

The oldest of seven, Lonnie eloped when she was 17 years old and I was 3. Her father drove her and her boyfriend over state lines to Maryland and signed for her marriage certificate then dropped her back at home. Soon she had our old apartment at 218 West when we moved to Taft projects. Losing Lonnie was hard for me. I hung the moon on Lonnie and now she was gone. She was the mother to all of us at 14 years old. Because of my mother's issues, Lonnie had been raising kids most of her childhood. Now I understand why she felt she needed to go.

WHAT I REMEMBER. . .

It is difficult to remember what happened first and last and how old everyone was. It was hard to hold on to my family then, and it is still hard to hold on to my family now. I was the youngest of 7 children, and there were people coming in and leaving our lives frequently. As children, some of us lived with our mother and others lived in other places. There was so much chaos.

My sister Larissa, third born, moved out of the house and in with her boyfriend, Robby, after high school. I remember taking pictures with them before they left for her prom. It was the first time I had ever seen anyone dress up for prom because she was the only sister that attended prom.

I think she broke up with Robby by the time she left for college. We visited her in Albany, NY. It was such fun sleeping on the pallets made with comforters and being around all of her cool college friends. I couldn't wait to visit again, but I never got the chance. Larissa came home to have a baby boy not too long after our visit. She dropped out of college, became a mom, and got a job.

MORE CHAOS AND CONFUSION

Keisha was number four, and I don't remember if she left before or after Larissa. She had to be about 16 when she had her baby girl, Ivey. It was not clear where she lived then. She came back and forth. After Ivey, she had another daughter a few years later. I was 10 years old when her children came to live with us. Keisha was on drugs and unable to take care of her kids. People would say things like, "Keisha is out here running the streets on dem drugs." Before Keisha's kids came, the "kid crew" was me, my brother, James, and my niece, Eva (Darlene's baby).

On my 10th birthday, we had a party. Everyone showed up and the kids played "Pin the Tail on the Donkey". Keisha knocked at the door, and my mom and her friends told me to bring them their purses from the back room before opening the door. Keisha seemed fine that day. We all danced and ate the lemon filled cake from Valencia's Bakery. It was a great party. I went back to my room to collect the money out of the birthday cards I had received. The first thing I planned to buy was a Rainbow Bright doll. When

THE PATH YOU CHOSE AND THE PATH THAT'S CHOSEN

I opened the drawer, the cards were there as I left them but there was no money inside. I walked out to the living room hot and panting to tell my mother that the money was gone. I stood there motionless as my mother yelled at Keisha to give the money back. Keisha yelled back, "I didn't take no money." She looked me in the eye before she left and said it again, "I didn't take your money." I wanted to believe her. I wanted her to stay and help me look for the money. Instead of arguing over it, the next week my mom took me downtown and gave me money to buy a Rainbow Bright doll. As time went on, phrases like "crackhead" and "go get my bag" always accompanied an impromptu visit by Keisha. I still wanted to believe she didn't take my Rainbow Bright money. I never saw her messed up or what I thought drugs did to you. She was always happy, talking fast, and ready to run the street. For a long time, when she knocked on the door, there was an immediate dash to grab my purse. Even if I only had a few coins in my purse, I was determined to never get robbed again.

Keisha would come and visit her kids for a few hours and complain about mommy not buying them new Nikes with the money she was getting from the state. She would tell them she would be right back and be gone for days or weeks. Some of Keisha's kids lived with us when she was on drugs while the younger kids were separated and went to foster homes. Social workers would come to visit and talk to my mother in the kitchen. When we moved out of the Taft Projects, we moved to Westchester County then Rockland County, New York. I was now in charge of Keisha's kids by the time I was in 7th grade. I was the new "Lonnie."

We moved every year for five years. In 6th grade, we lived in Georgia for a few months, then back to Harlem. My new school was Our Lady Queen of Angels. In 7th grade, I attended Kakiat Junior High School in Westchester County. In 8th grade, I went to Rockland County's Farley Middle School. I met some of my best friends there, and I even got to stay long enough to graduate middle school and go into 9th grade with the same friends at North Rockland High School. I finally had the same friends for about two years, and we did everything middle school girls do at that age. We talked about boys, caught the bus from route 9W to Nanuet Mall, ate in the food court, and went to parties. It was great whenever I was able to get out of the house and away from watching my nieces and nephews. Mommy wasn't working anymore, but she had to pick up her boyfriend in the afternoons from work and do all the errands that she wasn't able to do during the day because she had the kids, and I was in school. Most days I was babysitting the kids because they had something to do.

There Was No Protection

In 8th grade, my brother James was gone, and my niece Eva left years before that. My brother left shortly after my mother let her boyfriend Rodney move in with us. He was the kind of man that looked at 13-year-old girls like they were grown women. I knew the way boys looked at me and the way a grown man *should* look at a 13-year-old girl. Rodney would stare and stand in my doorway. I told my brother James and then my mother about his stares. When I was able to get her away from him, I told her how afraid I was to be left alone with him. Her response was silence, no hug or apology, just silence. I knew she was not going to protect me. She did not value me as much as she valued him. I wondered if she valued me at all. She knew nothing about me. She did not know my favorite food, and she didn't want to know. She did not want to know my concerns about her boyfriend. My mother didn't leave for weeks or months for drugs or drinking. She did not care. She, too, was gone.

THE PATH YOU CHOSE AND THE PATH THAT'S CHOSEN

One weekend, I visited my sister Lonnie in Harlem. I told Lonnie I did not want to go back home because mommy's boyfriend looked at me funny. I saw my sister get very upset and overheard loud words on the phone with our mother. She said, "I will call DCF" and "He has got to go." She was my hero that day, and I loved her for that and since then I always thought she was powerful. This much was evident. When I returned home, he was gone. I did not say a word, and nothing was said to me. My only thought was *I've got to call my sister Lonnie more often*. Two weeks later, he was back in the home. I asked my mother why he was here. She replied, "Is he doing anything to you?" Our already wounded relationship became irreconcilable on that day, and it has never healed. I hated my mother and now had to sacrifice more of my life for her happiness. I lost respect for her because she would have let all of us go for a man. A man she could not trust alone with her 13-year old daughter. I am not sure if trust was a requirement for her romantic relationships, but it was not present in ours.

After that boyfriend left, my brother James was gone, and I was alone with my mom and Keisha's kids. By the time I was in the 9th grade, a new man was living with us. He did not take my mother on dates, and they did not talk on the phone. His name was Larry. He was the ex-boyfriend of my mother's friend, Ms. Kerry. Larry was looking for a job wanting to get on his feet. He was initially introduced as a friend that my mom was helping. I realized they were more than friends when I saw them kissing in her bedroom. He was a roommate turned lover (at least that was the story I was given). Now, I understand most roommates don't share a bed. Initially, I appreciated his help with the kids. Then most of his talking turned into hours of yelling and screaming at the kids. His 40oz bottle of beer at the kitchen table became two then three 40oz bottles of beer at the kitchen table. His "occasional" drink became every night, all night drinking in a room by himself.

I was a 9th grader, tired of mothering kids, and I was tired of my mother's insistence on having a deadbeat man in her life. Larry, the new boyfriend, graduated from an in-house alcoholic to a man that wouldn't come home at night on occasion. A man that stopped being careful about the women he had been riding in my mother's car with all night. He was no longer careful about cleaning up after his joyriding. I missed the bus one morning, and Mommy had to drive me to school. As I sat in the passenger seat, I noticed a lipstick-stained champagne glass on the car mat. I picked it up to show it to her, and she said nothing. Many nights, Larry hurled profanity at my mother after long drinking sessions. He had every disparaging word to yell at my mother in the middle of the night, in her bedroom, in her house.

It was me, mommy, Larry, and Keisha's kids at home. In 10th grade, I finally had a tight group of friends. We all joined the step team afterschool, met up in downtown Haverstraw to hang out, and danced together at all the Jamaican parties in Spring Valley. This was the first time in years that I had the same group of friends starting the new school year with me. A few weeks after starting 10th grade, I was informed that we were moving to Virginia. I had already lost my sisters and brothers, I did not see them anymore and did not know where they lived. I was frustrated bearing witness to the screaming matches in the "house of horrors" my home had become. I was over being a full-time, unpaid nanny to three children. I was tired of being in charge all the time. I was the person feeding them, cleaning up after them, and bathing them. I did all of this after school while she hung out with her boyfriend. I wanted to go out with my friends and stay after school for clubs, but I had responsibilities at home. Now, I was losing my dear friends. The only thing I looked forward to was being away from home and hanging out with my friends. I was going to miss our walks, prom, and the bus to Nanuet Mall Instead, I was going to Virginia with a woman whom I could not trust. A woman who resented my constant awareness of her dysfunction. She was half-crazy, on Prozac, and her man drank himself stupid almost every night. At 14 years old, I knew way too much and had far too little power to do anything about any of it.

Well, at least I would have the bad kids, right? Wrong! Keisha's kids were "bad" because at 13 years old, three children were a lot to handle. Caring for three children is a lot to handle at any age. On the other hand, the kids were the only consistency in my life. They were there for me when the people who were supposed to take care of me were not. My mother decided to move to Virginia and leave the kids with my brother, Damon, and his wife in the city. So for a while, it was me and the crazy people that were supposed to parent me. Not long after moving to Virginia, Larry stopped coming home altogether. He preferred the company of other women and lived out of a motel in Petersburg, Virginia. My mother continued to visit him at that motel when she wasn't in New York City taking care of my ailing granny. During my sophomore year, I pretty much had the apartment in Virginia to myself. You would think I was sad and lonely, but by being alone, I got a break from drinking, hostility, and desperation. I came home from school, and I didn't have kids to feed or bathe. It was easy living only having to take care of myself. The only issue was transportation, and luckily, I made friends with girls that had cars. I soon realized that everyone drives in Virginia and that was a blessing. I was finally able to breathe, go to school, hang out with friends, and just be a kid. I found plenty of trouble to get into and trouble found me. As a 15-year-old with an apartment to myself and no adult supervision, of course, I found trouble.

No Room for Victims

By 11th grade, we had moved again. This time within the same county but a different school zone. I can't say I really cared anymore. Most of my friends were seniors and had graduated, and I just got used to doing life on my own terms. I wasn't breaking rules because I didn't have any. The relationship with my mother had been indifferent since middle school. We tolerated each other. There were not tender moments. I did as I was told, and she provided enough to prove she was not neglecting me. Whenever I asked her for something, she was apathetic and said she didn't have money. But months later she would spend over $1,500 on Christmas gifts. When she told me, she did not have money, it meant she didn't have money for what I wanted. I did not get what I wanted — I got what she wanted to get me. What I wanted was irrelevant. Even at 16, intuitively, I knew something was very wrong with her. Not only did I blame her for everybody leaving, but I also didn't trust her intentions. She seemed so uninterested in me, and at the same time, curious as to how others' opinions of me reflected on her. There was not a lot that I depended on her for, but there were some things I would not allow her to ignore. She was going to give me money for my prom dress. She was not interested in shopping with me or picking out hairstyles. She drove me to the store and waited in the car. My mother did not make a big deal over me. She enrolled me in a debutante ball during my senior year of high school. I did not have any interest in the program, but some ladies at church were putting their daughters in it, and she wanted to fit in with them. I was angry when I found out the amount of money she poured into that program. She was denying me money for things I wanted in order to impress other people. My mother did not take me to any of the debutant practices. She never even asked me questions about the classes we received.

By the time I was 17, I was the mother to my mother. I had to get her to take some responsibility for the choices she made. When my friends were being taught about boys, getting their first job, and learning to drive, I had the job of managing my mother. I worried constantly about my mother paying the rent. Would she spend this money on having fun with a new boyfriend? Was I going to be able to get new shoes before the end of the summer? I could not trust her to do parental things. I did not expect her to nurture me or be encouraging. I just wanted her to give what was due to me. I watched, waited, and chastised her if I thought she was getting ready to do something stupid with her money. Her doing something irresponsible with her money meant I would be teased about my run over shoes. It meant we were moving again because she couldn't afford the rent. I was going to make sure she used her money to take care of me even if she did not want to. Watching her meant I was taking care of myself. I became hypervigilant making sure she took care of my needs. I knew I was not a priority to her, but I was going to get what I needed. She did not have to like it. I was there to obey, and I did not have to like it. I was there to watch her and serve her. Obedience meant respect and respect was more important than love...that didn't mean I had to agree. I just had to do it.

My mom was the victim which meant I had no time to be a victim too. No matter how many times I told my friends, "Listen my mom is crazy," no one would ever really listen. They didn't have the power to do anything, even if they believed me. Often, dismissal and a "that's still your mom" is all I would receive. I knew I was powerless, a feeling I became way too familiar with throughout my life.

WE WERE ALL GONE

We were all affected by a condition, emotional toxicity, throughout my family. I am calling it chaos, confusion, mental illness, and trauma. I am naming the pain of never feeling protected. Mental illness sounds better than selfish, mean or making terrible choices. It sounds better, but it doesn't feel better. We never sat down and figured out where we all were. Why weren't we connected? Why didn't anyone take us to visit each other? We could have at least had each other. Although, I am not so sure we knew how to be there for each other. We had been disconnected so long we didn't know each other.

We never felt there was someone committed to us. We were on our own — ever worried about our survival. It was difficult to trust anyone. It was difficult to believe what was told. It was difficult to trust the world. This was the root of my anxiety. There was no time to explore who we were because who we were did not matter for our survival. Our identities were secondary to our usefulness. We were there to serve and do what was asked despite our feelings about the challenges, loneliness, and chaos. We had our separate lives in the same home, other homes, and placements elsewhere. It is strange to tell people I am the youngest of seven children and know that I don't really know some of my siblings personally. Some siblings I did know, and others I didn't know for long. We all have our stories about how mommy did not save us from something; how daddies were barely there or never around at all. There are stories about how some of us went into shelters and experienced our own abusive relationships. They were living their lives and I was living mine, and we were all lost. My family would have been the perfect family for intensive trauma counseling; we were all high risk. Intensive counseling for our trauma would have allowed the exploration of our family dynamics. We needed family counseling and support to create a safe space to process the changes of people being pulled in and out of our home. There should have been modeling and education about functional family roles and structure. However, this intensive counseling did not happen for us. The experiences created emotional toxicity which led me to detox and subsequent rehabilitation. It was not fixed in a few counseling sessions or with love or marriage. Cycles of toxicity, abounding chaos and a desire to seek peace led to a deeper awareness of myself and the impact of my experience.

It is difficult to remember what happened first and last and how old everyone was. It was hard to hold on to them then, and it's still hard to hold on to them now...

I grew up and accepted relationships ending as just a part of life; commitment to one another was optional and highly volatile. People felt unstable; there were no guarantees. I learned people would not hold on to you if it became too difficult. Today my family is disconnected. Some of us are still weaving stories together trying to make sense of what happened to us and all that we missed. "I never knew that," and, "That must have been awful for you," cannot suffice. Some patches will never be sewed, and some are just ripped out. It is just there, like an open wound, sore and unhealed.

5

The Struggle of Hope

ON THE SOFA

My only regret was not going deep enough. The first time "on the sofa"
my therapist was helpful and presented with limited emotional expression.
I never imagined her going home and wasting any time thinking about me
in between sessions. She was insightful about my feelings of abandonment
and the loss of my son's father. I did not dare expose her to the abandonment
of my entire life. Would she even believe me? Anytime I mentioned anything
close to my pain, people would hush me with, "Oh you should be grateful,"
or "You only have one mother." I learned early in life people did not want
to see your pain. Certain types of people received empathy, and I was not
one of those people. I found my comfort zone hiding behind the image of
"fun girl." I could completely disconnect from hurtful things when I was the
"fun girl." It seemed like nothing ever bothered me, and I always had a
snappy come back whenever pressed emotionally.

I should have processed a lot more in therapy. I should have talked about my low self-esteem. How I felt ugly since I broke up with my son's father. I couldn't remember ever feeling pretty. My beliefs around being overweight meant I would be limited in my options of men. I wanted to tell her about the things screaming in my head. Most of all, I wanted to tell her about my mom but I continued to scream in silence.

We don't talk about that. Our suffering is nobody's business or concern. These were the statements I thought about to justify my fear of talking about my pain. I left therapy with so much more to figure out. How was I ever going to be happy? Would I always be angry at my mother because she wasn't the mother I wanted? I wished she would have protected me. I would've told her about the boy in high school that came over and things went too far. I would have told her how much I had settled on those other boys because I didn't think I was pretty. While intensely fearful about not ending up like my mom and her drunk boyfriend, I overlooked all the ways I was mistreating myself. I wondered why my mother was the way she was and why I never felt loved unconditionally from her. It still hurt that my mother never asked me questions about myself. One day, I decided that I was going to tell my therapist everything. On that day, my therapist said, *"I think you are doing better."* I wanted to yell, *"But I am not healed yet!"* *"You don't even know what I have been through!"* *"Ma'am I have given you crumbs."* Instead of voicing my true thoughts and feelings, I smiled, thanked her, and walked out.

I would have several sofa experiences in therapy because anxiety and panic attacks plagued my life. When I was 30 years old and found a new therapist, I wanted to talk to her about my fears of becoming a licensed clinical social worker and a wife. I was finally going to be able to give my son, Zuri, the family he deserved and I never had. My career was expanding and I had to make some crucial decisions. Everything was coming together, except it wasn't. I wanted the therapist to tell me how to be a wife. I knew what I didn't want, but I didn't know how a family was created. How do I imagine a family I never experienced? I knew marriage was supposed to be a good thing. I knew people were always happy to hear about weddings and talked about their spouses. I didn't know marriage for myself, my necessities nor what I was required to give. It seemed like the right thing to do, and I was in love. And finally, after the years of education and stressful jobs, I was going to be licensed and have the opportunity to make real money.

I saw everything within my reach. Everything that I always hoped for was right there, but it didn't feel real or safe. A real family didn't feel real to me. I was the person that didn't belong. I didn't fit. I wanted this therapist to show me how to fit in the family that I wanted. I wanted her to assure me that this family thing would start feeling normal one day. Most of all, I wanted her to tell me this was real, and it was going to last.

The sofa was in a bright and cheery room. I met with the therapist and told her I met somebody wonderful, and I didn't know how to make a marriage work...how to make it work forever. I told her all the things I wanted were coming together for me, but I had no idea how to be married. Within three sessions, she told me I would be fine and referred me to a book called Hold Me Tight. I smiled again, thanked her, and read the book. It was a good book, about couples being emotionally vulnerable to each other. I still had no idea how to start doing that, "Be vulnerable." I had never seen vulnerable up close.

It was a few years later, and I was on yet another sofa. I was sitting with my new husband in marital therapy. We were just six months into the marriage, and I felt "unheard." My husband was a fixer. He had a solution for everything. He was seven years older, and he had been married before

Initially, I felt lucky that he was so mature and knowledgeable about everything. He had a plan for everything. I felt lucky that I was with a man with a plan until I started to feel "unheard." More of our conversations went from sharing ideas to him telling me the plan. . .which was his plan. Soon it felt like my thoughts, feelings, and instincts were muffled by his plan. It was hard to feel like someone's partner in life when someone tells you that you are wrong. I fought back trying to debate and became resentful when I was ignored.

Our first time on the therapy sofa together we were asked about the best parts of each other. There were so many best parts despite our conflict. He still felt supported, and I still felt protected. I learned that men think differently from women and that I had to be mindful of my words because they hurt his pride. The snappy comebacks and one-liners were not helpful in my relationship. My power was in verbal aggression. I used hurtful words to defend myself when I felt attacked or unheard. Growing up in Harlem, a good cuss out was an event where we watched and learned. I also learned that the man you date may not present the exact same way in marriage. When we were dating, he would ask me all kinds of questions and we would talk about ideas all night. He was so curious about me, and I loved that about him. Marriage was not an extended date. It was really quite different. I learned a lot in marital counseling, though some of those things may have been basic communication skills, I didn't know them. I didn't grow up with a father or brothers; my father died, and my brothers left our home. I needed someone to explain the dynamics of a man. Men weren't like a woman with different genitalia. My lack of understanding made it difficult to explain to someone who did grow up with a man in their life. There were unspoken rules, and subtle themes that I did not understand.

By the third therapy session, I thanked my husband for coming to marital counseling with me. I told him I had never felt closer to him than I had when I was talking to him about us. By the fourth session, the therapist challenged my husband on some of the ways he was attending and responding to me. At the end of the session, he smiled at the therapist and we left. On the way home, my husband told me that he was never going back. He said that nothing was wrong with him, but if I needed to go talk to someone then I should. I knew it was pointless to process this with him. He was not asking for feedback; he was giving his declaration. I was back to feeling unheard.

I was on the therapy sofa by myself over and over. Once and a while, he would throw out a manipulative "carrot stick." He told me, if I got better, he would eventually join me. I would receive the occasional compliment when I surprised him by responding in kindness. It would soon be overshadowed by statements like, *"It's not going to last anyway."* Once again, I was in a relationship with someone who was emotionally disconnected. He kept his promise and never returned to marital counseling. I stopped feeling safe with him. I was trying to communicate better. I wanted to love and trust him, but it felt like I was walking on eggshells. He never asked me about what I was working on in therapy, and it seemed the marital issues were squarely planted on my shoulders. My problems were mine alone, and he did not need fixing.

The first year of marriage was the hardest. The first year of marriage my heart was broken and the man I married was no longer there. Soon after his refusal to go to marital therapy, I was rushed to the emergency room. I had the worst pain I ever felt in my chest. For a year prior to that date, I was having all sorts of health challenges; this included severe panic attacks while driving and headaches in the middle of the night. They all started the same way; my heart began to accelerate and wake me up. I felt nauseous and weak. I crawled to the bathroom, stripped off my clothes, and got into a cold shower. On many nights, my temperature spiked, and I felt my heartbeat thumping in my head. When the attacks occurred more frequently; my doctor told me that it was stress and high blood pressure. My husband thought it was a good idea that I quit my clinical manager job and figure out some work that was less stressful. After a few months, I agreed to quit. It was getting harder for me to do anything.

On a summer night, after midnight, my husband drove me to the ER. My blood pressure was sky high upon arrival, and I was in unimaginable pain. A few hours later, an ultrasound revealed that my gallbladder was inflamed, and I had a rare tumor on my adrenal gland. I was diagnosed with a pheochromocytoma; the tumor had been the reason for most of my symptoms of panic, night sweats, and exhaustion. My primary care doctor missed this diagnosis for nearly a year. My husband was in the room when the doctor explained that the only treatment for this tumor was medication then surgery. The doctor also gave us hope; telling us that I could stop taking blood pressure medication and conceive after my surgery. We had not been trying, but it was good to know. My thoughts and fears were whirling around in my mind as I laid in the hospital bed. Repeatedly, I told my husband I was terrified, but there were no other options. The alternative was fatal.

Similar to my pregnancy, I wanted to be held even tighter. I was scared out of my mind. I wanted his presence and words to reassure me. For the weeks leading up to the surgery, we were in a different place. We walked around the house barely acknowledging each other and trying not to disturb the other. Our tensions were already strained and then this news. Just days before the emergency room visit, we had our first real marital fight. We were seven months into marriage, and our loud voices hurled criticisms and insults. He ended that argument by yelling, *I will just get my shit and leave!* My mind didn't know what to handle first; my husband wanting to leave me or my possible death. Both options seemed just as painful.

My whole life was different. I wasn't working but instead going to the doctor every two days to have them check on my heart. I was also taking medication to slow down my heart rate, which caused me to be tired and fatigued. Prior to my diagnosis, I signed a lease for an office for my private practice. Like a Raisin in the Sun that dream was now deferred.

I was stuck in this marriage where I felt unheard and in a body that was not functioning. Then, I had death looking me in my face. I found myself in and out of my body constantly. Emotions flooded my mind, and I was drowning from the weight of my current life; it seemed unreal. I was scared and numb all at the same time. My husband and I didn't talk about these feelings; instead, we only spoke when necessary.

Finally, my body was ready for surgery. We arrived at the hospital early in the morning. The nurse explained so many instructions to me. The level of fear within caused me to become speechless. My husband was sent out so I could be prepped for surgery. The nurse assured me that he would return for a short visit before I went back to the operating room. As time passed, I began to think about my death even more. My anxiety was high. To make matters worse, a doctor came in and explained that he had to place a PICC line (peripherally inserted central catheter) in my neck. This precaution was taken in case I had an emergency and needed medication during my surgery. I asked when my husband was coming back for our final visit. The nurse informed me that the time for visitors had passed, and the surgeon was ready to operate. I began to shake with fear as the doctor placed that line catheter in my neck so the surgery could commence.

When I woke up, my husband was not in my room. We saw each other briefly before he said he had to go pick up my son. My husband decided not to come back that night to stay with me in the hospital. I was traumatized, and alone in a hospital room. The next day, I was discharged and in a lot of pain. I could barely walk to the bathroom or sit up. I wanted to be at home recovering. I did not want to waste any more time resenting him.

My first night at home was quiet. He cooked dinner, and I was happy to see my son for a little while before the pain killers took effect. I woke up hearing him get dressed around 6 am. He told me he was going to the gym and offered to bring me some breakfast. I was still half asleep and declined. A few hours later, I was awake, and he was still gone. I waited that entire day for him to return and for food. I could not walk down the stairs; I couldn't do much. I laid in the bed with anger and hurt. He took 10 days off work for family medical leave, but every day he was gone, finding things to do to get away from me. My son would come home and make easy mac, applesauce and whatever snacks he could get together for me. When I was strong enough to sit up, I confronted my husband about his neglectful treatment. It was an angry exchange, which ended with him suggesting that I should be grateful that he is still here.

During this time, I reflected on my health issues and how I planned to start a private practice. I wanted to help people, but now felt lost and filled with despair. According to my husband, my problems could be solved by simply listening to him about how I should feel.

LOVE, MONEY, AND BORDERLINES

Just a few years earlier, I met a wonderful man with no debt and an absolute desire for a life and future with me. It was what life was supposed to be; I was going to be a wife. I had $56,000 in student loan debt, a mortgage, credit cards, and no idea how to manage money.

I was anxious about money and another person involved in my money. Single never married, I wasn't knowledgeable about managing money as a couple. I assumed he knew how things were supposed to be because he had been married before. He reassured me that he knew, what he was doing.

In no time, my diminutive savings was gone. You can sort of assume what happened with a relationship full of vague boundaries and secret money beliefs — not to mention trust issues. Some of you may have already experienced the strain of the vagueness, lack of communication, and underlying trust issues. Remember what I learned in childhood about depending on other people...don't. The lack of a collective plan and emotional baggage soon overwhelmed our relationship. I felt so connected to him in marital counseling, and when we reached the 4th counseling session addressing his behavior, he quit. It only reaffirmed what I learned in childhood; I could not trust anyone.

We didn't have very much conversation about money other than "if you need something let me know." My husband never said no to anything he wanted or wanted for me. His paycheck was for him to enjoy after paying bills. He would save but only for larger purchases. The bills did not include my debt when I was out of work with health issues. We didn't talk about my debt, his spending or a lot of other uncomfortable things. I wasn't sure if it was anxious avoidance, but I didn't talk about money. It was traumatic just recalling the childhood of "not enough." Why would I want to share that with someone I loved? It felt like just another barrier to loving me. I never shared, and he never really asked.

After months of going to marital counseling alone, I missed feeling that connection to him. He got angry whenever I attempted to talk about uncomfortable things. He argued with me until I acknowledged that he was a great husband. Again, I was the one with the problem. He never said he was perfect, but if he had a problem, he would be the one to take care of it. Most nights I was waking up at 2 a.m. to cry.

It was the night before my 33rd birthday, and we had been in silent treatment mode for maybe two weeks. I was depressed and ruminating in pain most days. We got into an argument when he left the house. When we came together, I broke down and began sobbing. I told him how unhappy I was and about the late-night crying spells. I told him how I felt alone all the time. I told him we needed counseling, and I wanted our relationship to be different. He looked shocked at the display of emotion, and he remained quiet. His next words were, "I will look for a place tomorrow."

He always gave mixed messages. For example, a letter describing how much he loved me on the day he signed his lease. He would tell me he would always take care of me and then remind me that he had his own place and expenses now. He started threatening me with moving out maybe seven months into marriage after a very heated argument. I sort of picked up on the fact that when he didn't like something or get his way leaving was his default. His response only reinforced my fear of abandonment. It was a really confusing time and the messages about love were ambiguous. During our marital separation, I continued to receive mixed messages about love. When he signed his second-year lease, my fog began to lift from severe depression. I knew I wasn't going to live through another year feeling mixed up. I went looking for answers.

There was more clarity for me after communicating with the other woman he was dating. All the manipulation, gaslighting, and resistance to counseling made a lot of sense. He told me he loved me, and on the very same day perfected his online dating page. It wasn't the first time that I couldn't trust someone I loved. My attitude wasn't the issue and listening more wasn't the issue. I talked less and less and then my voice was gone. The fights were not the issue. If you stop talking, there is nothing to fight about. He didn't like anything, my voice, my friends, my family, just me Cheating is terrible, but I may have been able to deal with it if it were not for the emotional wild goose chase he introduced. I was more than hurt, I felt he played with my emotions. Here I hoped for a better relationship while he was in another one. I resented him for manipulating me and giving me hope. It would have been kinder to let me go; that I could have understood. Realizing that I had been sent on a wild goose chase for a husband that did not exist drove me crazy.

That's what kept me so angry. . .the running and riddles. The chew toy of "hope" that was thrown out for me to fetch only to run back and for it to be throw away again. The reality that this man was never going to be the husband that I needed finally settled in, and for that, I am most grateful. I acknowledge my part; I had no idea how to be a wife and knew very little about marriage. I never considered what I required in a relationship. All I knew was someone loved me and would love me forever. I needed love and it felt overdue. I didn't bother myself with the details of a life together. I appreciate how hard it is to tell our truth. The truth about my husband hurt. I wasn't being loved. I was being kept crazy and quiet about everything I felt. It felt familiar.

A couple of years later, we were preparing for a divorce. I found myself on another sofa. This therapist got right down to it. At my initial assessment, I talked about my childhood and relationship with my mother. I felt overwhelmed with feelings as I remembered all my attempts to love people and keep them around. She listened intently. At the end of our session, she gave me a book titled, *Borderline Mother*. She told me I would understand once I read it. I was set to return two weeks later. During those two weeks, I was engrossed in the book, truly amazed by how much it captured my life. For the first time, I was able to identify the relationship I had with my mother and see how it was so connected to the relationship with my husband. These two people would say to my face that they loved me and yet had no idea what their love looked or felt like for me. I felt unheard and hurt.

Their behavior consisted of lying, manipulation, isolation, perpetual victimhood, and a lack of accountability. I felt crazy about asking them to reciprocate my love. It was my job to take care of them by consenting no matter what. Anytime I used my voice, it felt ineffective. What I wanted didn't matter. Things were perfect as long as I didn't say it wasn't. When the imperfect moments occurred, it was never their fault.

I LOVE YOU, BUT I AM NOT GOING TO LISTEN TO YOU . .

30 YEARS AND SEVERAL SOFAS LATER...

Each decade of my life has brought some challenges. I survived a pretty stressful and bleak childhood. I was born into chaos. My mother was overwhelmed with her life while trying to parent 6 children by the time I was born. She lacked the emotional capacity to create healthy attachments. My mother was not at all connected to her body, mind, and spirit. She was there but vacant. Alive but not living. There wasn't a safe place for her to fall. This left no place for me to fall either. My mother was unpredictable.

I never knew her, and there wasn't an expectation that she should know me. She gave birth to me and provided food and shelter. She treated me to birthday parties and Catholic school. She fulfilled her responsibility, and I shouldn't expect more.

My 20's were filled with the stress of being a single parent while working and fighting through anxiety. There was always a fight. I found myself constantly having to get into the ring. I fought with my son's father. I fought to finish grad school. I fought for love and attention. I fought for someone to affirm and help me survive.

In my 30's, I lived through the wonderful haze and ideals of marriage only for it to end in divorce. That season literally set my journey in motion. This is when my awakening began. I was not sacrificing one more year or decade to the whims of chaos, rejection or discontent. Finally, I was going to figure me out. I didn't exit their lives to hurt them; I left to stop hurting me.

After years of waiting to be validated by love, I was swept off my feet. I knew I would finally have a forever and always. Then, I realized someone's love doesn't heal all things. It was like waking up from a coma. I learned people can only love you as much as they can love themselves. People can hurt you a great deal because they have been enduring a great deal of pain. It took years to talk about the pain. It took even more years to speak my truth. When you do muster up the courage to speak your truth, say it aloud. The mere sound of the hurt starts the healing process.

I am now able to tell my story. I can see life's bigger picture and all the connections along the way. I don't know if "hard" really exists or if it's just a process of becoming.

WITHOUT YOU, NONE OF THIS WOULD'VE BEEN POSSIBLE

I have a very strange appreciation for the people that hurt me. I have this saying, "Without you, none of this would've been possible." They are part of an amazing story and journey. It was not easy, but I fell out of love with things being easy and just accepted that loving people would be hard. I wasn't going to let hard stop me. This included love.

It's remarkable to go from a powerless child to realizing your own power. The dream is beautiful when I think about it. When I want to stop, because it's hard, I think of my legacy and my grandchildren. What will I want my great-granddaughter to know about me? She won't have to wonder because she can read this. The one thing I want her to know is that I never stopped. It's not about likes on social media or making a ton of money. I never stopped being pulled to a passion with intention. I held space for the hard things, especially love. That is enough. That is a lot.

I began to think about my son. He was my experience of true love. His love for me was unique and unmatched. It was hard to trust that kind of love. I had to give what I didn't have. I lacked emotional stability. Loving felt like finger painting in the dark...messy. I had an image in my mind about what love should look like, but the lights were off. No instructions had been given. Occasionally, I felt like I hit something. Fortunately, it didn't stay dark forever. I remembered that I had the love and support of amazing people and God, with that my sight returned.

6

Grace is Sufficient

Love is patient, suffers long and is kind, unselfish, does not envy. Love bares all things, hopes all things.

1 Corinthians 13

I knew I didn't have that love.

Realizations months and years after divorce were insightful. I always wondered why my husband didn't reach out and comfort me when I was sobbing that night. I told him I was unhappy. Trying to figure out all the reasons someone hurt you may take a lifetime.   I think this was the first time he ever heard my truth. He heard me angry and sarcastic. He heard me lie and tell my friends that everything was okay. He never heard me vulnerable, asking him for something emotional. He told me he thought I was happy because he stopped hearing me complain. I wasn't happy I was just quiet and stayed out of the way. It was my dysfunctional familiar. My voice was gone, and he was unbothered when I was in silence. He hardly said anything anymore. It bothered me years after the divorce how comfortable he seemed in my silence. Anyone who knows me will tell you that I love to talk! I love meeting new people, socializing, and playing most of the time. So, for him to think my silence meant contentment confused me. I don't believe he was thinking much about me. He stopped asking about me, so how would he know?

My broken relationship was a key to greatness. I was working through a lot of pain, rejection and confusion while treating clients and crying spontaneously in the bathroom at work.

I felt powerless. The family of my dreams felt like a cruel illusion. I was lost. The icing on the worst cake ever is that I was left alone to explain to my son what I had no explanation for — that his new Dad was not coming back. He wasn't supposed to leave. My son wasn't supposed to see me wounded. I was supposed to make my husband go to counseling, become self-aware, and affirm me. I was supposed to fix it because I was the fixer. It was never fixed and that also meant something else was wrong with me.

My son Zuri didn't get sad, look scared or ask me any questions when I told him he wasn't coming back. Zuri was protective of me in that way. One day, I was going through my son's phone, and I saw a text he sent to his friend about his stepdad moving out. My heart broke all over again. I lost hope that this was just a terrible dream. Brokenness can be a great asset for a therapist when it has time to be processed and healed. I didn't have time; I was overwhelmed and couldn't hold on to anything. Sitting in therapy sessions felt like Novocain in my body. I felt nothing for a very long while.

So, I already knew I was giving up my dream, my love, my marriage, and now my private practice. I couldn't work, and it was hard to wake up. Some days for sure I didn't get up. I was facing the short sell of my home at the height of the housing crisis. My mortgage was due to double, and the home was worth half of what I had paid for it. My income was unstable with temp jobs, and I lived with packed boxes downstairs for when the time came.

REDEMPTION OF THE ABANDONED

For a long time, I blamed my husband for being so mean and cruel. I blamed him anytime something didn't work out for me. For a long time every statement started with, "If he would have just. . .If he would have just come to couples counseling. If he would have just trusted me…If he would have just loved me." One day, I looked at myself and said, "If I would have just. . ."

If I would have just focused on how to love myself and allowed love to follow. If I would have just realized how valuable I was and held on to my own voice. If I would have just learned to accept people for who they are and not allowed animosity to build when they weren't what I wanted. If I would have just paid attention to the awesome and dynamic changes that were occurring within and not changing the other person. There was such a different way of looking at life now. I was slapped in the face with God's love while going through all this. It was not a spiritual awakening; it was a spiritual reckoning. I worked so hard at everything, being a mom, social worker, and wife, and none of my work resulted in what I wanted.

Just as I was losing everything, the real peace of God's love appeared as if it was always there. I realized there was no work that I had to do for God's love. I had no full-time job, no money or husband. One night I was crying and later woke up with the belief that everything would be okay. I also knew everything would be different. I wasn't going through all this without a transformation. I still struggle with love just being unconditional. There was no checklist or qualifiers, it just is.

I never did lose my house; the mortgage company offered new terms. My son and I were able to build an even more authentic relationship. I didn't really work at a thing. One opportunity was given, then another, and so on once I accepted love couldn't be earned.

Today, I get to do what I love working from home. I am home after school every day to greet my beautiful son. It all came together with love. It's the journey I fight to stay on.

After a multitude of amazing ladies' nights, so much time in therapy, and reflecting, I figured out my new voice. Let's recall that scene in the movie Get Rich or Die Trying when 50 Cent is recording a song after being shot nine times and he notices how much his voice sounds different. His girlfriend agrees that his voice is different but that his voice was better because she could hear his pain. I had a beautiful new voice baptized in pain.

"Being broken and trying to sit in the pain of others in counseling, meant staying in a novacaine like experience. I felt numb for a while."

In all the chaos and confusion, there was simultaneous grace. I quit my initial grad school program when I was pregnant. I was accepted into the social work program at VCU. The second-year was comprised of long days, 8 a.m. classes and 7 p.m. classes, research projects and statistics class. I was struggling with school, and I was also struggling with motherhood.

One evening, I stood in the lobby of my son's daycare mumbling to myself about not having a sitter for the class that night. It was one of the many days I wanted to quit. I was tired…tired of classes and papers and deadlines. I was tired of getting diapers and finding a sitter after the daycare closed. I was just tired.

Right before I walked out of the door, an older lady that worked in the daycare offered to watch my baby so I could go to class. She lived around the corner, and she was taking care of her grandson who was a couple of years older than Zuri. I offered to give her something, but I really didn't have anything. I was living off of student loans. Every week she babysat my son so I could go to class. Every week I would offer her something. Every week she told me to keep my money and "just graduate." I graduated that spring with my 2-year-old sleeping though most of the graduation. I wish I could remember her name. She was just one example of having exactly what I needed exactly when I needed it without doing anything to deserve it.

The day my friend found me crying in my bedroom, I was pregnant, confused, and desperate to feel found. I was lost and didn't feel attached to anyone. I was all over the place, and my emotions were spiraling down. There was nothing to hold on to. When I felt like letting go, she walked in with peaceful energy and made it okay to just cry. I called the next day and made my first therapy appointment. I needed that appointment and to sit on that sofa. I realized what I really wanted to do. I wanted to be on the other side of the sofa. I wanted to figure out people. My experience of sitting in that intimate space with someone and sharing my pain changed the course of my career and developed my purpose. I knew I wanted to connect with people in a space of emotional intimacy. Even in so much pain, there was grace.

Although I found myself in an agonizing marriage filled with emotional abuse, the timing of grace was so perfect. I married this man just before a tumor was discovered in my body. Despite how things ended, someone was there for me. He worked and paid bills when I couldn't. I had insurance and medication because of him. Someone was there to pick up my son when I couldn't. I had no idea that I would need anything, but God knew what I needed. Some things were meant to happen but not meant to be.

When the marriage was ending and my private practice was due to close, all I did was pray for a job with medical benefits that would offer me time to be at my son's games and stay active in his life. Grace showed up again, I received a letter from the mortgage company offering a no-fee refinancing option. Someone also gave me a job posting for a behavioral health telephonic work from home position with an insurance company. It's ridiculous this thing called grace. I received more than what I expected through repeated acts of grace.

Through grace, I found compassion for myself and others. I felt how difficult it was to truly do the right thing and stand on your truth. Even in those relationships that I thought I would never recover from I became more aware of a deeper meaning of love. The best gifts during my recovery were people sent into my life to deliver a message of reassurance that everything was going to be alright.

One random day during my marital separation I felt the spiraling again. I went to work and somehow let it slip that I was headed for divorce, and my husband was in a relationship with someone else. It just all seemed to spontaneously erupt from my mouth that day. I wanted to take back all my oversharing and redo the entire day. It was immediate silence with a coworker and I alone in the room. A few moments later, he expressed how sorry he was, and we spent the next hour talking about his guilt and shame from his infidelity and later divorce. Who would have thought that I would be in a room with a man on the other side? I learned that day that there was another side, and it wasn't completely selfish and hate-filled. The other side was in pain. Listening to him express his remorse and talk about his own self-esteem issues helped me in ways he won't ever understand. I couldn't answer all the "whys," but I understood then that there was more to the story. He gave me the apology I needed but never felt. Love and marriage are complicated and whether you are 2 years or 32 years in, you are still figuring it out.

Grace showed up for me as a mother. I came from a family broken and disconnected both physically and emotionally. I was always afraid of being alone. Zuri came into my life just shy of my 23rd birthday. My entire pregnancy should not have happened. His father was not my imaginary husband. A single mom was not the life I intended. My fear was being alone and that is exactly how I felt pregnant and single. I wish I could say that there were some belly and foot rubs, but there weren't. I wish I could say we never argued and did everything to make sure the baby didn't feel all the fears that we felt but that would be a lie. It was rough! A lot of tears, loneliness, and rejection. As I studied human development and the vulnerability of our brain to early trauma, I was so engaged in intentionally loving my son.

My son welcomed me into unconditional love. When I was worried about everything I was doing wrong, he gave me the kind of love that makes you confident even when you have nothing on your resume. He showed up and said, "You are my most important thing." It took a while, but eventually I believed it. I loved being someone's most important thing. It felt special, and most of all, different. He never stopped loving both his parents. It didn't matter how at odds we were, Zuri always came back to love us. Nearly 18 years later, I am still learning how to love through him. He is the greatest sign of grace and the greatest gift from God.

7

Love, Money & Freedom

I wanted it all. The life that I hoped for when I went to visit my 'white family.' I wanted a comfortable home in the suburbs and a husband that had an important job. I also wanted enough time to enjoy it. I was going to take my son to football practice, and we would cook out on the grill on weekends. For many years, I found jobs that I hoped would provide the money and freedom to enjoy my loved ones. There was no one who wanted to win in life more than me. This was a struggle.

MY JOB FROM HELL. . . SATAN INCLUDED

After almost 2 years of working in public community services, I had an unsupportive supervisor and decided to look for other employment. A former coworker informed me of another public agency hiring. He encouraged me to apply. I was about 6 months from completing licensure in social work and the new position offered to provide clinical supervision.

My new job started at 7:30 am with a PACT team meeting. At meetings, we reviewed every client in the program. It wasn't long before I noticed the degrading and sarcastic way my manager would speak to almost everyone. She scolded employees like you would a child. There wasn't a plan to train me or even provide sound clinical supervision. Every day, I'd wait for her to confirm a meeting, to review my role. Those meetings never happened. Most days, I drove around with seriously mentally ill clients from one place to another. In my first week, I called my bestie Tishsa and said, "I think I made a mistake." It was hard to believe that someone would want to leave a new job so soon. The energy in the workspace was oppressive. It was toxic and sucked the life out of me. I could not imagine working there another day and the thought that people would want to retire from such a place was simply incomprehensible. That place was a plantation. There weren't any lunches with coworkers, chatting in the snack room or small talk about your weekend. The people there excelled at staying busy and looking busy. I was up you know what's creek without a paddle. Every day I wanted to rip that badge up and throw it in my manager's face. Every day I thought, "I am broke and have a baby." I had given up a job that was kind of bad for a job that's hell. I began to literally refer to myself as the runaway slave.

For weeks, I drove clients around with no lunch break. I ran every kind of errand possible and never ever heard a "thank you" or "good job." I knew I was going North. As I planned my escape, a higher up came to visit each member of our team including me. Privately the higher up let me know that he was part of an investigation involving harassment. Apparently, a member of the team made a formal complaint against "the devil," aka our manager. The complaint alleged that "the devil" referred to a coworker as "inept," "slow," and "incompetent." Yes "the devil" would often call her and other coworkers derogatory names in our daily team meetings. I didn't consider myself a snitch, and I didn't have any friends here. This wasn't a workplace where people were happy to see you. No one seemed to socialize in or out of the office. We perfected minding our own business and avoiding the devil. I was in my mid-20s, and I had never worked in such a hostile environment. I had mounting anger for the coworker who actually referred me to the devil and damned me to hell. I approached him in the hallway one day and my exact words were, "What the hell?"

GET OUT!!!

His response was, "Ignore the devil, she is all bark and no bite. She is a great manager." Has anyone ever told you something so untrue that your body just responded on its own? I just shook my head and literally walked away planning my escape. I saw another coworker. He was one of the few who didn't smoke cigarettes every hour to numb their feelings. I asked him where he had worked before this, and he told me Philadelphia. We both looked at each other with the "How did you end up here?" gaze. He blurted out, "The devil is the worst supervisor that I've ever had." It was as if he was reading my mind. He said our jobs were hard enough working with people coming out of mental institutions after 10 or 20 years. After a short pause, we both said in unison, "I gotta get outta here".

I didn't care how long I had been there. I did not care about a gap on my resume. I was going to find my freedom. I couldn't even believe that my former coworker was a "slavery wasn't that bad" type of person. People tell themselves what they need to hear in order to abandon their dignity. It sickened me! I was in a twilight zone resembling hell, and I wanted my life back. Laughing and making jokes at work was a necessary treasure that I needed to find. I wanted to enjoy my days off and I didn't want to spend 2-3 hours after work talking about the job from hell.

My health was declining. Most days, I didn't have time to step away and have lunch. Most of my food came from the 7-11 I visited before or after appointments. We weren't allowed to eat with clients. I was always with clients, so gas station food was my only option. I got tired of being hungry all day and just packed snacks in my purse.

I was constantly speeding to appointments with clients, picking up clients from the hospitals, and dropping off meds. There was not one hour in my day designated for a break. It was challenging to get a bathroom break because I was always on the road. I tried to avoid truck stops and gas station bathrooms as much as possible.

Aside from the poor self-care and toxic environment, our work was intensive. Our clients were high need and at risk for rehospitalization, homelessness, and the criminal justice system. In a typical day, you were convincing someone to take their meds, pleading with a landlord not to evict, coordinating temporary housing, getting someone food, and talking with the nurse about medication side effects. I thought about all I learned in social work graduate school, reflecting on the whole person and how stress impacts mental health. I was working with people who taught self-care while neglecting myself. I was about 3 years into my social work career and had encountered poor leadership, oppressive environments, and unrealistic self-care and working conditions. There was bias, lack of resources, harassment, and no real tangible way to stay healthy or rich. All these conditions present in social work jobs were ironically hypocritical. Yes, I was making 18k more than my first job in Child Protective Services, but it really didn't feel like it. My entire weekend was rehabbing from the week of work. It was the worse job I ever had.

I requested a few hours off from the hell job. You would think this wouldn't have been a big deal. Unfortunately, it was because my role was so extensive. My absence meant someone else had to deliver meds, fight evictions, and everything else they did for their own clients. I took that time off and used it to interview for another position. I leaped out of hell with my first offer due to desperation. After 90 days of hell, I spent my last day saying goodbye to my clients. At the end of the day, I walked into the office, took off my work badge, cell phone, and keys and told them this would be my last day. I handed them my resignation.   Unfortunately, the devil was already gone for the day, but it didn't really matter. I was free. The look of shock on the faces of my coworkers said it all. Some thought I was joking, and other's faces screamed, "How dare she." They asked about two weeks notice. I just looked at them and thought "We are in hell, and you want me to give notice." Virginia is a right to work state. You can be fired or quit without notice. I already knew the devil was vindictive. This was evident by the harassment investigation. I wasn't giving her two weeks to torture me in hell.

I can't say I ever had a job that compared to hell. There may always be issues in leadership, communication, and balancing work demands, but it's never been hell. I always tell students who are interested in the social work field about the hell job because I want them to understand how toxic environments affect us. It's harmful to our health. The impact of stress on this one job changed my mood for all of life's activities. Yes, working on a PACT Team with seriously mentally ill adults was very challenging, but I didn't quit because of the work. I quit for reasons most people quit. You quit your manager. There was no appreciation of the lost lunch hours or hours spent driving in a hot car with clients that may have poor hygiene. There was no debriefing about stressful situations and encouragement for self-care. I was the machine that completed billable tasks. My humanity was completely ignored.

When morale fades and turnover is high, the agency loses in many ways, especially revenue. All the productivity lost, the time to find a new candidate, then to interview and process a new employee. All this results in fewer services for vulnerable clients. Clients lose a lot, and there were pangs of guilt about leaving them. My clients and I deserved to live full and healthy lives. The agency didn't set up a culture where that was encouraged. Clients had workers coming in and out of their lives. Frequently, they were being moved around to someplace else. They will need to retell their story and start a new trusting relationship once again. If I am having issues, whether personal or work-related, I need a safe space and accommodations at work. There is no perfect job but there is a culture that may allow your greatness to come forth. Whether that means having the time to take a college course, sign up for leadership training, train for a marathon or even write a book. A job should support you in areas of your life; it should not be your life. I am a much more focused worker when I have my personal and creative energy paired with my desire to do well. Simply put, working should not be a struggle.

. . . AND THE DEBT

Aside from the 6-year journey of college and earning a master's degree, it was the blatant fact that, years into my career, I was still very much struggling financially. I was 20 something, and after the hell job and a few hard-fought jobs, I was left wondering, "Is this it?". I decided to move back to my mom's house so I could save money for a home before my son started kindergarten. It was a move stemming from a complete spirit of surrender. I did not plan to stay long. I would work hard and maximize my savings. My mother and I continued to have a strained relationship, and I underestimated the emotional stress, angst, and frustration I would encounter. I had a child now and was back in a place full of all the childhood stressors I once faced. I felt stuck, and I saw that my plan of saving was swiftly derailed by the stress of my living situation. Soon, I realized every single week I was still in the hole and never seemed to have anything saved. I just gave up. My home buying plan was pushed back every month. I felt stunted and I knew it wasn't working. I spent more time at bars and restaurants avoiding home.

There was always stress at home. I am not here to judge anyone who shares a home but coming home to a toxic situation was not at all healthy for me. I had a very toxic relationship with my mother. I wasn't the best mother I could have been and remained worn down most of the time. After about a year of living in my mother's home, I proclaimed that I would never come back. I knew it was time for me to go. I had to save myself again. Khadijah to the rescue! Here we go again.

I left work one day and walked in a mortgage broker's office and told them I wanted to buy a house. I had absolutely no money and had no knowledge of homeownership. All I knew was that I needed to get out.

It wasn't until later that I realized all my decisions centered around money or rather the lack of money. I went to grad school as a single mother because I was going to make more money. I stayed at the hell job 90 days because of money. I lived with a toxic person because of money. As altruistic as the notion of social work is, I was disillusioned by the idea of trading my time on earth to work for basic needs. I couldn't afford to do what I wanted, to create, and to explore. The rush hour commutes, getting my baby to school, after school care pick up, then tons of paperwork created a feeling of busy yet not productive. It wasn't what I had hoped for and with all I owed in student loans and bills, I couldn't see a way out.

Money is an essential factor in our struggle, closely connected with health outcomes, mental health severity, and life expectancy. No, money is not everything, but it's easy to make that statement when you have some money.

As my salary increased, money was still directing me. The idea of having a great impact on the world and being directed by wages was mismatched. I did a little bit of what I loved and a lot of what made the most per hour. I needed the money. Money was a tool for family vacations, soccer cleats, doctor's appointments, and awesome Christmas memories. Most importantly, it was the key to options. I wouldn't have to stay in a hell job working long hours or missing school trips if I had money.

Scrolling through Facebook, I read a post about working 16 hours and getting overtime money. I knew of people making 3x more than me, and they were still directed by money. The race never seemed to stop. Today, I am directed by the value of time. After the money is established, it becomes a fight for freedom. That is where a real battle begins. Am I chasing money or chasing financial freedom? Money and freedom welcome new struggles!

AFTER THE MONEY IS ESTABLISHED, IT BECOMES A FIGHT FOR FREEDOM.

The fight for "work-life balance" keeps the most coveted jobs occupied. I discovered that coveted jobs were not necessarily the highest paying. More of my clinician friends are working in fields where the new work week is 30 hours or 4 days a week. Independent contractors are replacing full-time positions. Now telecommuting and working from home have drawn people to really look at freedom of time as a measure of compensation.

According to the US Census Bureau, the average commuting time for work is 4.35 hrs. a week, 200 hours a year. There is also the additional time and expense of childcare and family care needs. People want to spend more of their time being more available to their self-care needs and quality time with the people they love. When people don't have to choose between their work and their family, loyalty tends to grow. We need more than a paycheck; we need to be well. The sooner you create your wellness requirements, the less likely you ever end up in hell job. I was in a hell job for 90 days; some are in a hell job for 30 years. Until we value our wellness, companies have no reason to change their culture.

SELF-CARE, WHO CARES

There is no better way to heal from brokenness than to address self-care. Self-care is a fairly new term used to describe behaviors that support health and overall wellness. Taking care of self in a profession focused on getting clients to take care of themselves is essential. It's no debate that having less stress will improve most situations. Whether finances, work or family, stress has an impact. What if we expand the idea of stress and really explore the connection of mind body and spirit? Treating the whole person has been the new direction of health, healthcare management, and mental health. This is not just hopefulness and advice that better nutrition, exercise, and supportive relationships will make you feel better. This entire concept of wholeness and integration of mind body and spirit is evidenced-based. We can look at the Adverse Childhood Experiences Study that suggests strong relationships improve the adverse outcomes of children. Supportive parenting, communities, schools, and even supports and resources for the parents improve both medical and health conditions. The Essentials for Childhood Framework [5.5MB, 44Pages, 508] proposes strategies communities can consider to promote relationships and environments that help children grow up to be healthy and productive citizens so that they, in turn, can build stronger and safer families and communities for their children.(www.cdc. org). Even beyond families and communities there is an awakening occurring right now about human needs for health and wellness. This is a time where friends, colleagues, and I are really questioning the entire concept of how we live, respond, and sit in the fullness of the world. Communities of people are questioning not just how we have raised children to be "seen and not heard" but also roles in marriage and families. We are figuring out how we want to live and what kind of living is optimal for us. Perhaps that's why the 40-hour work week and school calendars are being replaced with laptop lifestyles and homeschool co-ops. Self-care impacts everything. . .even the way we have relationships with others and ourselves. Self-care creates a space to at least question, "Is the life, work, and demands working for me?" There was a time when I — along with many others out there — didn't consider the quality of life. I am sure many people at my hell job weren't concerning themselves with life optimization. We were raised on survival mindsets. The mindset proposes that as long as I am alive, I am making it, and when I die, I can stop trying to make it.

But not today!!! Self-care and self-awareness would cause us to question all the experiences we choose to bring into our lives as well as the time it takes to devote to those activities and assess how valuable these activities are to our sense of fulfillment.

I will question everything! Is making dinner where I want to spend my time resources? Do I want to take on a new project? Is this a relationship deserving of my very valuable time and energy? Some may feel it's over-analytical; however, not caring for yourself results in high rates of adverse health conditions, poorly rated quality of life, social isolation, and financial woes. So yes, process exactly what you need from life and be intentional about your time. Do you realize the shift that would have occurred in my relationships, my health, and my money if I would have taken this approach early in my life? No one becomes sick, broke or sad overnight. It's every single small decision that adds up over time. The same goes for becoming healthy, rich, and mindful; it's every single decision about how you are going to care for yourself.

I mean it, take a moment and look around. How close is your nearest fast food restaurant — the kind that offers quick, cheap, and processed food from a drive-thru window? Fast, easy, and cheap has become the mantra of society. We rush through everything. Realize that your diet is everything you take in, not just food. We hurry through school to get to college, then rush to find a job. It's a great option to take your time and consider you.

No one becomes sick, broke or sad overnight. It's every single small decision that adds up over time.

Burnout, overworked, and underpaid! Nearly 50 percent of American workers felt that they were in this position, https://news.gallup.com/poll/109618/Half-Americans-Say-They-Underpaid.aspx. We can wake up and consider what is truly fulfilling. We must think of what is keeping us healthy and well. The alternative is keeping our heads down and being told what to do, how to do it, and when to do it. Obviously, the latter will have its downside in that 52.3% of Americans are unsatisfied with work. https://www.forbes.com/sites/susanadams/2014/06/20/most-americans-are-unhappy-at-work/#509b079c341a

And no, I don't think everyone is lazy, nor do I think that half of Americans are in hell jobs. Perhaps some are uninspired and feel confined by their role or it's just bills and survival. This type of work, social work, should not only be the job that you choose but the job that chooses you What if we expand our self-care practice to impact our clients, family, and community? We already have the tools to impact with passion. In order to make that a reality, it's going to take a plan and a strategy to optimize the work that we do directly with clients, communities, and policymakers. Our wellness is tied to the impact on the world.

Assessing Our Self Care

Before we do anything anywhere with anyone, we need to assess our own self-care. We are not going to have long and effective careers if we aren't healthy enough to come to work. If you ever had an encounter with someone who was experiencing burnout then you know you have received some of the worst services ever. No one wants to be that person. Even that person doesn't want to be that person.

We are socialized to follow and following isn't a terrible thing. Following without awareness is dangerous. Self-care is a term used in our field to describe the need for people to take conscious and deliberate steps into awareness. Self-care supports not only our mental health but our overall health. Self-care is connected to prevention and management of health. A huge part of my role in healthcare is creating a space to address self-care. And I am still amazed 5 years later, what we put in front of taking care of ourselves. The issue is usually, "I don't have enough time," and, "I don't know how to take care of myself." I am often talking to people in their 40s and 50s who have not considered the care required to be at optimal wellness. Most manage basic hygiene and an annual physical. However, there is so much time given to work, childcare, and other responsibilities. This leaves an extremely small box for self-care. I am not talking about the awareness that comes with meditating 45 minutes twice a day. I am talking sleep, nutrition, exercise, and exploration of interests.

Who told us, "You are an adult now, fun, comfort, and enjoyment will have to wait until the kids are 18, 21 or retired." Who said thinking about your care is selfish? Is giving to yourself automatically taking from someone else? As a therapist, I have to battle the automated black and whiteness of life in a therapy session. I must challenge the idea that someone did something bad to you so you must be bad. Challenge the idea that someone did something bad so she must be bad. When we pull back the layers it becomes much more complex. You didn't cause that bad thing, and sometimes bad things happen. Even good people do bad things. It's a lot of heavy lifting to get someone to come over to the land of gray. Our feelings and perspectives are very different. That difference comes from our culture, upbringing, experiences, spirit, and values.

Practicing awareness requires shifts in mindset and the ability to look without judgement. Simply following someone may present an easier path. It requires a lot of work to be aware. It's the trade off if you follow you get to belong, but you may give up your ideas. On one hand we admire the renegade, the self-made man or the entrepreneur, and on the other side of that hand, we don't feel stability with a person trying a new thing. That's why there are still so few renegades or superheroes. Prioritizing self-care and unconditional love in a "worth proving" world, may lead you to a wilderness where you feel isolated and alone for a time. We are made to feel that we don't deserve it because someone said so. Someone recognizing your worth doesn't mean it exists, nor does the lack of recognition mean you are worthless.

You ever hear the expression, "Doctors make the worst patients"? Apply that to social workers. We have some of the worse self-care that's mostly due to wanting to save the world. How did I even survive my brokenness while treating the broken? Debilitating panic attacks, a rare life-threatening tumor, a childhood of disconnection from my mother, abandonment, heartache, and a divorce I survived. I treated myself with the very opposite of what life had given me; I gave myself compassion. I humbled myself enough to learn how to be the mom that my son needed. I analyzed why hurt people hurt me. I explored my value, wholeness, and beauty. I learned that I needed love, forgiveness, and awareness.

I realized through my work that many clients were ending up in hospitals because there was no support, no loving relationship or no community awaiting their return. People were becoming suicidal and disconnected from life and themselves. We are so disconnected from our bodies that we sometimes have to be reminded to do things that we need…like eat or breathe. Yes, take a deep breath and full up your belly. Aren't you already feeling better?

I cringe now when I think about all the horrible fast food, overwork, high stress, poorly managed existence I once had. It was damaging, but I was so unaware of my mind and body connection. I was stressed out and rushed most of the time, and my diet definitely reflected what I was feeling. I was eating my feelings. Even today I must really stay connected to being overwhelmed and eating because of anxiety. I want to fully give and work in my purpose. I can only do that if I am well.

It's challenging for anyone to make the shift to focusing on the life you want. So often we are so focused on holding on to what we have that we stop thinking about what we want. Without that shift, we stay in that comfortable mode just holding on to what we know. Expanding our minds beyond comfort is applicable to many areas of life. It's a challenge in our society not getting roped in with group thinking and actually create beyond what is seen. When I was in my struggle, all I could think about was paying a bill and getting above water. I didn't consider being financially stable enough to not worry about bills. Everything I told myself was created. I wanted just enough money to pay bills, so I earned 'just enough.' Later, I told myself I wanted to have quarterly vacations and that was created.

Your bills may be paid but what else have you accomplished? Everyone has their own talents, skills, and weaknesses. I am giving myself room to explore or support new ideas around work, money, and lifestyle.

Money a Symptom and a Tool

It doesn't matter how much money or how great the plan, if the relationships in your life are off so is everything else. In my thirties, I saw how money was indeed a tool. I almost lost what I thought was everything, and it was transformative. My relationship with money and everything else changed.

Growing up in poverty, things were constantly moving and changing. My money mindset was filled with anxiety. In mindfulness spaces, it is believed that thoughts become things, and so it became. I didn't think I would ever have enough and never had enough. It became my entire identity. I never had enough money, never felt loved enough, never felt enough. But that lack mentality did not go away. I lived in fear constantly that I would not be able to take care of my son. What if he had to move every year because the rent went up. What if he had to say goodbye to his friends every year and be the new student every year? I had come from poverty and now lived in debt which to me is worse than poverty. Poverty is zero versus debt which is negative zero. I knew I had to change.

Money is hard. It's not the money, but all the mental work needed to keep it in its rightful place. For those reasons, I don't glamorize entrepreneurship, self-employed or even employment. Everyone's journey needs are different. My focus is on living the life you want to live. When my fear of lack became reality, I lost focus on my work. I couldn't help people heal when I was broke and broken. If you are not deeply connected to purpose, you are simply creating your own hell job. It's important to stretch yourself but not to the point where everything else in your life diminishes. We are here to have life more abundantly not just money.

One day. I started thinking about money. I searched on YouTube, "How do I become wealthy?" I was met with a stream of self-made entrepreneurs, online classes for real estate, and other promotions. I started to *knowledge gulp* money. Some things were simple, and I knew I could do right away. I began making a budget. I compared my income and expenses and created financial goals. It sounds weird to say, but I actually looked at my income. I was so traumatized by the idea of not having enough. I felt paralyzed and never really looked. I was supposed to be a 'whole strong black woman.' I felt the opposite. I felt confused and insecure. I had to get some control and order in this part of my life. I faced that spirit of fear.

My employer offered a work from home option which meant reduced expenses. I made use of some great employer benefits to bring more money home. My income was now what I use to consider rich! I began to enjoy my earnings and took some pleasure trips with my son. I began my plan to become debt-free. I started with the Dave Ramsey plan of baby steps. I attacked my credit card debt, then my car was paid off in a little over a year. However, the big kahuna arrived, $56,000 in student loan debt. Now for some reason, I could not get my head around this number. It was a huge number, and I was growing weary of tracking and noting my checking account. It felt obsessive. I also got tired of working 2 jobs. When I needed to, I rested. When I had extra time, I worked more side jobs. I stopped focusing on not having enough money.

It was the habits that I changed that made me feel more stable. When I changed those habits, my money improved. What I did with the money helped me feel rich. I still worked toward being debt-free, and I also considered how I was living my life. I realized that I wasn't really motivated by money. I was motivated by time. I was able to do what I loved and able to spend time with loved ones. I was excited to see my son come home and tell me about his day. I loved volunteering, mentoring, and reaching out in my community. Money frees you up to do what's best for you in order to have the most impact in your life and on the people around you.

MONEY FREES YOU

So, I imagined some new goals. I wanted to expose my son to more of the world. I wanted to travel more. I wanted to serve others in a way that changed lives. I wanted to retire well and before 65 and be debt-free. During this exploration, I mentored with the Association of Black Social Workers. Talking with students in social work helped me realize that some of them would face the same challenges in this field as I had…low pay and high burnout. It can be such a rewarding field, but the social work brand needs to change. Overworked and underpaid is not ideal for any profession. I truly believe you cannot live your best life to others in a condition of lack and stress. We need to be rich enough to give in every way. If you can't afford to give, then you are not truly successful. When you can give, it adds to your wellbeing. The idea of being a giver means you have enough to give.

I realized how much my lacking mindset stole from me. I was always broke, so I never planned to travel. I never shopped around for an international flight, just assuming I wouldn't have enough. I became creative about solutions when my mindset shifted. The mindset of lack and money trauma ensured that I stopped exploring. My excuse was I was on my own and these bills were not going to pay themselves. I totally stopped factoring in myself when it came time for new clothes or treats. There wasn't enough for me. I didn't have enough, and I wasn't going to ever make enough. Even when I had more money, I created the "lack of" mentality repeatedly. The more money came in, the more money escaped. I was committed to lack. When my thinking shifted, money seemed to accumulate. A budget offered me accountability. Tracking anything allows you to look at yourself. Psychologically, you spend less, eat less or anything less because you must acknowledge your actions. Educating myself about money provided changes and new goals. I had to develop other streams of income — working smarter and not harder. I learned to live on cash. I revamped the saying, "A car note is a terrible thing to waste."

GROWTH – CONSISTENCY OVER TIME

America has 43% of the millionaires in the world. In fact, 1 out of 20 Americans are millionaires. Americans are millionaires due to the economy and money invested over time. That means 5% of the population are millionaires by investing in something over time. But let's ponder the alternative, 95% of Americans are not millionaires because they are not investing consistently over time. There is nothing wrong with not being a millionaire; however, there is nothing wrong with being one. If given the choice, which would you choose? I know which one I am choosing. I want to be that 5%. I would have conversations with people talking about money, and my whole body would tighten up. I hated being financially unstable as a child, and I hated feeling defeated about money as an adult.

So, let's go back to the facts, even though investing is a proven way to get to millionaire status, most people will not invest. People living in poverty are not able to invest. If you can go on vacation or buy lunches at work, you have enough to invest. Even when I made significantly more, I didn't invest or save. I had the same money shame with more money that I had with little money. When my psychological shift occurred in my relationship with money, my money changed.

We already know healthy foods, exercise, and rest support good health, yet healthcare costs grow every year due heavily to poor lifestyle choices. There is hope that investing effort over time will improve most facets of your life; like your marriage, career, and parenting. As the great Les Brown says, passion will fade over time, we must have the 'why. We must treat the "why" first. A million dollars seems really far away for most. Many people will not realize the many small shifts and changes that add up to 1 million bucks. We also don't truly value the opportunity of time. Time creates money and money requires time. An investment can start relatively small. The number matters but not as much as we think because of the time. Consistency compounds the money. A debt-free household of $50,000 creates a great opportunity for growth. That's a lifestyle with travel, investing, and success. The younger me would have ascribed a person's financial success to their intelligence. Today, it's clear there are some brilliant broke people. We all have access to information and that is not enough. The people engaging with consistent actions become successful. But again, that mindset of lack often hinders exploration.

This money thing is not all about 6 or 8 figure incomes. While learning how to get my money together, I got myself together. I had to confront my money trauma and fears. My entire childhood and early adulthood had connected money to lack, instability, and shame. I wanted to learn to have a different connection with money. I witnessed family members fall out of a relationship because of money — that was my first indicator that it was powerful. I had gone to court a couple of times over money with a family member and someone I considered a friend. I hated that feeling of stress and conflict. I challenged the mindset of lack. I wasn't going to be limited by the title of social worker. I was going to be an author. I was going to be a creator. I wasn't going to limit my income, travel or anything that I valued. I am going to live up to my values and that was going to be the best life for me.

I read books about money principles, purpose, and spiritual growth. I began to study all about my money shame and all the beliefs I needed to unlearn. Anything that felt true I kept. I know that my mindset of lack controlled my money decisions. My new mindset of abundance will control my future decisions. Everything that we do is connected to something inside of us. This is hope for you right now to start creating the beliefs that feel whole for you.

Money Mantras

1. **Never Borrow Never Lend**- This applies to relationships of any and all kinds. The only way to avoid those awkward moments, tensions, broken relationships, and possibly litigation is not to borrow or lend in the first place. My money is a gift, so I give only when I am able to gift it. When you give a gift, you never wonder what happened to the gift years later. My only intention was for them to enjoy it for its purpose. That's how I want my money to feel, enjoyed and purposeful! Think back to the money that you have loaned or borrowed. There was no enjoyment as both of you were worried. Stressing about paying it back and never getting it back. Anxiety and distrust were triggered simultaneously. If my money can't be a blessing, freely given, I don't want to give.

2. **Process Money Trauma**-Trauma is often the result of an overwhelming amount of stress that exceeds one's ability to cope or integrate the emotions involved with that experience. A traumatic event involves one's experience or repeating events of being overwhelmed that can be precipitated in weeks, years or even decades as the person struggles to cope with the immediate circumstances, eventually leading to serious, long-term negative consequences. I was exposed to repeated events of being overwhelmed by meeting basic needs.

I moved often and was pulled away from friends every year. Growing up in poverty caused me to have a desperate kind of relationship with money. Becoming a single mother, meant facing the burden of financial responsibility. Money was complex. Everyone needs it, and yet asking for a loan, child support or assistance may lead to an incredible amount of animosity and resentment. Money causes people to treat you differently, brings jealousy, and may end relationships. Money was connected to my childhood of chaos and confusion. Money seemed so unpredictable, and even at a young age, I can remember my mother placing her money anxiety on me. There was never teaching about budgeting or financial goals. Money was unpredictable. I was a child anxious about my mother's spending. I didn't trust her to do the right thing with money. As I became an adult, I acted out the trauma. I never really paid attention to money. I was confined to working a lot and not having enough. I reinforced this in thoughts and actions. My change came about when I thought about my son. I didn't want my Zuri to wonder about my competence with money. So, I just kept my ignorance hidden and used credit cards. I didn't want him to worry as I worried. I wanted him to trust me with money. Eventually, I sat with him in my truth, and I shared all the ways to avoid debt and be intentional about life.

Even as I earned a higher income, I continued to embrace the mindset of lack. I continued to increase my expenses without a plan or budget. All the while saying I want my son's life to be different. I had to define "different." I had to make financial choices that were in line with my goals. Generational poverty is learned just like generational wealth by adopting a set of values connected to actions.

3. **Money is not good or bad**- People with money aren't better people. People without money aren't bad people. People are valuable because of who they are. Money is a tool to care for yourself and others. Money isn't the only tool to care for people.

4. **Financial Prosperity is not Shameful**- More money is not greedy. Its purpose is to grow your dream. Bigger dreams require more money, more time, and more focus and strategy. Feeding 10 people requires more than feeding 2 people. Expansion honors your values and serves even more people. Don't allow anyone to make you feel guilty that you added more to your life through hard work and vision.

5. **Embrace a wealth legacy**- Over the last few years, I had abandoned the idea that debt was necessary. I was able to adopt new money behaviors when I thought about what role money would play with my legacy. I proclaimed this would be the last generation of debt. Generational wealth would be passed down. We will invest in short and long-term goals. We will not fear money any longer. I envisioned my great-grandchildren learning how to invest because their great grandmother started. I wanted to leave a legacy in more than just money. I wanted to leave a legacy of who I was in the world. I want to be remembered as a person who enjoyed life and shared herself with people. My grandmother had amazing food buffets when her grandchildren visited in the summer. I love that legacy. There are so many advantages to being born when I

was born. I graduated college earning 2 degrees, and I have every reason to create a legacy. My grandmother and I are not statistics.

Being legacy minded means living in a way that expands beyond just me or my needs. We can all create a legacy — access to information, free education, free libraries, and the love and support of someone.

Recently, I sat down with a friend about finances, and we shared some of our money traumas. We talked about retirement and having a plan for our families. He mentioned the stress of being behind on some bills and added that he was taking 3 vacations in the next 6 months. He also bought a new car in the last year. My awareness in just hearing this bought up a hint of anxiety. "I can't judge anyone's journey," I repeated in my head. However, this is a classic example of increasing lifestyle, increasing debt, and increasing an abundant appearance. I asked him, "Why take 3 vacations?" His response, "Vacations are an investment in self-care." The idea that anyone thinks you must take a vacation to take care of yourself was alien to me. I think of self-care as a daily practice. I find joy in sitting in the park or mindfulness in nature just a few miles from home. Telling yourself self-care is an expensive investment is a belief meant to be challenged. Trust that I didn't waste my time warning him about financial pillars and credit scores. A lot of people have adopted the "life is short" way of thinking. Perhaps life is short, but a legacy is forever. We should all be enjoying life. However, I can relax anywhere when I know my needs are managed. I had to keep reminding myself that I am legacy minded. I am also not married to convenience. I am committed to my passion and that sometimes means discomfort. Discomfort is often the path of awareness. I must challenge my discomfort to build awareness and self-discipline. If you have ever fasted for about 3 days, it's uncomfortable. Without food, you notice so much more of your environment. You also realize just how little food you need. Your fast doesn't need to be food. Try going without any comfort like TV or social media. You will find that you have a considerable amount of time to learn new things. It challenges you to reconnect with face to face relationships. It may even deepen the intimacy of your relationships.

6. **Never judge someone's money experience**- When I started learning about money, investing, and personal development, I started listening to motivational greats like Les Brown, Zig Ziglar, and Marie Forleo. I couldn't wait to share. I would tell friends, family, and anyone I could. I soon noticed a conversation about money was like bringing up a venereal disease. People just felt that should be a private conversation, but not me, I wanted to learn more. Money brings to the surface people's money trauma. Sitting with that trauma is a challenge. I know I just reviewed my friend's shockingly opposite money mindset. However, I could have won an award for all the stupid stuff I did with money. I probably didn't have a lot of friends encouraging me to get my money managed, but I don't know if I could have seen past comfort and my own pride to make any changes. I bought a car several years ago with a warranty for an additional $5,000 and it covered a tire patch, which saved a whole $30. I used my college refund money to fund my sneaker collection. Yup, I am paying back loan money for sneakers I wore 20 years ago. But probably the worst is that I married someone without having one intentional and specific conversation about money. I also proceeded to start a business while deeply in debt. I've been there and done that.

Most people were not taught how to manage and care for their money, so we tend to follow the crowd. Inside of this sort of money fantasy is the desire to look financially secure. Great clothes, hair, and vacations fit the fantasy. Life will happen, with an illness, job loss, or divorce. You and your fantasy will be jolted back to reality. Money is a journey, and people have to decide when the change happens or if the change happens. Focus on you and be honest about your mindset. If legacy is not where you are, then it's not. Money is extremely emotional. Give yourself the love and time to become what you want to be with money.

7. **Money mentors**- Open up to new people and ideas when you are developing yourself. You will need people who understand your vision. I cannot over emphasize the value of information. Your mentors may have diverse views, and you can choose the parts or paths that speaks to you. There are so many people I know who live frugally, and I adore them and the simplicity of that kind of goodness. I also embrace the people who create a life of travel and exploration. I celebrate the 40-year-old retired employee with a million-dollar net worth. I also celebrate the 30-something start-up business owner who is scaling their business to provide more amazing services and content. Part of my gratitude is accepting that there is more than one path in our journey and wherever you are led is ultimately right for you. Mentors inspire me and help me feel connected to my goals through our shared experiences. Mentors remind me that there is so much opportunity. Just think about how many hamburgers joints we have, and they are still in business. I was a huge Dave Ramsey follower when I initially started connecting with money. It was so helpful in paying down debt and exploring my spending. Why was I buying more and more and then saying I didn't have enough? No mentor — other than Marie Forleo — creates a better space to consider your gifts to the world. I love her because she helped me expand the idea of having a business and life that I love. The fact that she worked seven years to build her empire reminds me of the reality of patience in legacy

building. I'm even more impressed that she worked various jobs to support her dream. This resonates with me as someone who works side jobs to fund my own dream. For many people, investing money in personal development is a step they are not ready to take. Considerable time and money are needed for personal development. There are great mentors out here for development and financial empowerment. I have discovered Ramit Sethi's I Will Teach You to Be Rich and Thomas J Stanley's *The Millionaire Next Door,* which offer great information. I have grown to love a podcast "Choose Fi" to explore a lifestyle not dependent on exchanging time for money.

8. **Challenge your idea of fun and money**- Have fun wherever you are. Don't depend on money for your fun. People won't like this because I feel we are far too unconsciously wasteful of time and money.

Let's go back to my friend. We will call him Sir Cashalot. Sir Cashalot proposes that multiple exotic vacations are essential for self-care. According to his thinking, expensing fun is the way to care for ourselves. Is there anything free that he could do for self-care? Why yes! Is there anything relatively low cost that is also considered self-care? Why yes! I have expanded my definition of fun to include: passion driven, purposeful, fulfilling, relaxing, aligned, and engaging. There are so many ways to explore fun for $5, and it won't take away from your financial responsibilities. Fun, relaxation, and self-care are essential. If you take expensive vacations then can't afford retirement, you are not caring for yourself. Overextending yourself financially creates more stress, then you need more vacations to escape the stress…and so on and so on.

I enjoy my life daily. I enjoy my life because I understand that peace is present within and not at a destination, so it's everywhere I go. Travel is great because you can choose what you want to explore, but peace is free and everywhere. I love the idea of travel just not more than the idea of saving or investing. All of it is important and you have to figure how to have all of it in your life. If you are a priority you won't compromise your health, goals, wellbeing or money. Funding your fun but not funding your freedom does not connect with me at all.

9. **Giving is part of who I am**- I accept that my purpose is beyond myself and will even be used to touch people I haven't even met. No matter how resistant to giving you may be, I realized I never went broke giving too much. Now, I have gone broke from not paying attention, not planning, making choices to impress other people, and fueling my ego. But never ever by giving, even when I had very little. I would give and somehow a week later a refund or a bonus or a new project would arrive. God assured me of provision. Giving is always connected to everything, and it has never resulted in lack. I am blessed that I have never faced long-term unemployment. I always had to look for the right kind of work. Most people would describe me as dependable. A lot of my work had been word of mouth referrals not the classifieds. So, working has allowed me to give and giving has allowed me to live the life I desired. Giving is a financial and spiritual legacy. Giving not just of money but also of self is crucial because generosity attracts giving people. My mindset of giving identifies who I am today. It's replaced my 'lack mindset. If you are rich enough to give, then you are rich. I began using Marie Forleo's mantra, "There is more of that [money] where that came from." It is really crazy, money showed up when my focus was giving. I am always happy when I give. I am was never happy loaning or borrowing. . . got it!

10. Gratitude- Money will never become stressful if you embrace every dollar with gratitude. Whether it's your dream home or a delicious sandwich, I recognize that money is being used for a specific purpose. *There is more where that came from* acknowledges abundance of your lived experience and intention at that moment. Every year I made more, more bonuses, more opportunities. I am grateful to be able to do what I love, living the way that is much kinder for me. Gratitude created a path of recovery in the struggle. When you value your minute and your dollar as a small step, more seem to find you. It is what you do with the little that determines how you manage more. I have more minutes and more dollars. I am so grateful for the experience of poverty because it helped me dive deeper into the emotions of money. When it comes to money most often people will not follow facts, they will follow emotions. If everyone followed facts, we would all be investing at birth. We would be delaying gratification to grow money. Money is not just about interest and currency. Money is often an expression of how people felt about themselves, their relationships and their trauma. It was a mirror to how I felt about my lack and my loss.

I know money can't fix it, but healing fixed my money. I stopped identifying myself with instability and lack. I declared that I was more than enough. I was abundant and everything changed. Money should not be feared; it fulfills important needs and desires. It also reveals a lot about us.

The feeling of saving a 6-month emergency fund was audacious for someone from poverty. I had never reached that level of stability. There was a sense of pride knowing that I did this on my own. This accomplishment helped me to affirm that I could do much more. There was a real awareness. I was able to relax, knowing that I had some security for emergencies. Security is a feeling many single parents desire. I was grateful that this was the most I had ever saved in my life. I participated in automated savings, and it wasn't anything I had to think about. I am a person who is successful when I don't have to make a lot of decisions. When an action becomes a habit, it doesn't require as much time. One accomplishment led to another. I changed my 401k contribution from 4% to 16%. Retirement was important since my 20's but I could not bear to see anything taken out of my paycheck. My mindset was instant gratification not growth. My goal now is debt freedom, and I will continue to pursue the best ways to achieve that status. What's a small goal you can start today? Can you bring your lunch 4 days a week? What talent or skill can you market? When you become creative about creating wealth a lot more options are available.

MAYA ANGELOU SAYS, "SUCCESS IS LIKING YOURSELF, WHAT YOU DO, AND LIKING HOW TO DO IT."

Most people will have to fund their own dream with the understanding that, like most investments, it won't pay off for many years. Yes, success is the equation of consistency over time. It's the ideas that you formulate and challenge during that time. I felt a responsibility to my son — to provide him with childhood experiences that were imaginative and fun. I created a life for him that was full of experiences. He traveled, took martial arts, attended acting camps, and went to summer camps. I believed he deserved a life full of exposure. The exposure would help him grow and get to know the world. In the last few years, I began asking, "What do I deserve?"

I had lots of passions, and I loved spending a little time with each of them. I knew I could have more, but I needed an intervention for myself first. I needed to go back and explore those limiting beliefs. Limiting beliefs about who I was, my abilities, and what I was here to accomplish. I deal with my mindset of lack by telling my son he could have anything if he worked hard.

I wanted him to believe he could do anything, but I was stuck between my desire to create and my obligation. I wrote down lots of thoughts and ideas and continued to fail forward until I believed in my vision. Mindset is everything, and it needs to be continually fed, challenged and supported internally and by amazing people around you. I had a lot to overcome from childhood sadness and relationship brokenness. I needed to find a way to look at my life and legacy differently. Even having the idea, that there could be more is still a challenge. The only reason that I was so persistent was that there was someone to inspire. I was bottling ideas so long I had to birth some just to make room.

Managing love, money, and freedom may be overwhelming. You will have to confront the most difficult part of life...change. Whether change is for the better or worse, change is a challenge. Unconditional love changes things. Love should be our motivation to change anything. The one thing I heard over and over from people in recovery was, "I have to learn to love myself." It's hard to hurt yourself when you love yourself. First, you will have to let go of the judgment that says you will be punished if you change. Then you will let go of your fear of failing. You will fail and that failure will be your teacher. My goal is lifelong learning.

Adopt a new identity into unconditional love. This is the kind of love that can't be taken away when you act in a way that is less than yourself. We have inherent value and purpose and our job is to live in that purpose. Think about all the people who helped me along my journey. For example, my first therapist or the lady at the daycare center. They were part of my journey in becoming a therapist and even sharing these stories with you.

Everything is part of your journey even the people who didn't intend on offering kindness and love. My son's father and ex-husband offered some painful realities of relationships. I experienced abandonment, yet without them, I couldn't have met this new sense of compassion.

8

I Don't Have to Fight

Every dream requires something from the people in your life. Whether it's patience or a time to talk things through, those things matter.

You need your tribe. You will want to quit. You will get tired, discouraged, and probably feel really dumb at times. Therefore, having those special people around you is key. You must tell them what you need. You must set some time away to just nurture them. They love you, and they want the absolute best for you. If that is not the case, leave now.

As my marriage was ending, I was at the height of burnout. Everything in my life was burnout. I needed someone to tell me how to live without chaos and confusion. I was tired of being obligated to expectations.

When I challenged death, I realized my own value. I examined my life. Did I tell my people how much they meant to me? At 31, my medical scare opened me up to reflection. I endured an incredible amount of physical and emotional pain over the next few years. Several years passed before I was ready to be grateful for that kind of pain.

The gift of compassion is difficult to recognize and even achieve. It's not just what you will see show up in your life. It's how you'll respond to anything that shows up. The gift of grace will open you up to the reality of loving yourself completely, even the parts of you that you can't stand and won't name out loud. Grace will allow you to say aloud, "I love myself." You will be able to bring it into your awareness. This is who I am, and I can choose to respond differently. Life is different with self-compassion. You will be gentler with yourself. You will experience the fullness and balance of yourself. This won't be artificially puffed up pride that says, "I am special, and no one is like me." It's more like, "I am connected to everyone and that helps me in being in more of a connection with myself." It's a journey you are taking with yourself that other people help you uncover.

You will be triggered because most people will not be living in awareness of who they are and the power that they possess. You will remind them of the power that they have been trying to ignore. Someone will make negative assumptions about you. They may even degrade you. You will feel unheard and unwanted. You will want to fight back and seek revenge. Hopefully, you will take some time and sit with those emotions. You will think about the fearful place they are coming from. Hopefully, you remember the amazing power within and how it challenges the weaknesses in those around you. The freedom you walk in every day reminds people their chains are mind made.

You can't dim your light or minimize your power, which will cause conflict. You will take the time to connect and do what is right. At times that right thing may seem really lonely. It will require more time and patience to find other people like you.

It is the time of life discovery. My possible death opened up an entire new life. My faith was changed. I wasn't just in life to endure pain. I had to accept God didn't want me in pain unless it was for a purpose. I wasn't a martyr for other people. I was here for my purpose. I began acknowledging all that I lacked. I didn't have a strong family foundation. I didn't have a long and happy marriage. The only thing left that I could challenge was my limiting beliefs.

If you find yourself in a space that feels unchangeable, it's because you haven't challenged yourself. I am better at everything in my life when I've challenged my beliefs. The more I cared for myself the more care I received from others. I began to become intentional, asking myself, "How does this feel?" Yes, I have to remind myself to stop and feel all the time. Coming from a past where I had to be disconnected from emotions in order to survive, emotions were confusing.

Vision and faith are amazing. They may also leave you tired, overwhelmed, and anxious. Challenging anything means standing in the unseen. If I told you to cross an invisible bridge and guaranteed that you would get to the other side, would you go? That's where I went wrong, I wanted people to see my vision, and it was invisible to them. Only I could see it. After failing to persuade people to see my vision, I tried to get them to desire my vision. Finally, I waited for people to be excited for my vision. I was disappointed waiting on the emotional feedback of other people. I was accused of being ungrateful or complicated.

Be prepared the attacks will come. Group thought and societal norms make people feel safe. Different ideas challenge their sense of safety. Don't let it distract you. The vision you have must be celebrated, nurtured, and desired by you.

ADDICTED TO STRUGGLE

You will expend so much energy working against the current in the river. Does this mean everything you want will be easy? No, however it doesn't mean it will always be hard. Have you ever met someone who really wanted something? Perhaps they wanted a big shift with money or an amazing romantic relationship. You notice your friend working really hard trying to figure it out on her own. You may offer her thoughtful and loving advice, and she dismisses it. Repeatedly, you offer her advice as you keep watching your friend hit a wall over and over. You know that your feedback is coming from a loving and genuine desire for your friend's best interests. You really want your friend to win.

At this point, you must step back and consider this. If someone really wanted to win, wouldn't they do anything possible? You would at least seek some information and or support to help you in this process. If advice is reasonable, proven, and supportive and there is a true desire, change would happen. A saying comes to mind. The student always finds the teacher. People who are connected to their desire find what they need.

I believe many people are addicted to struggle and are more afraid of their wildest dreams than their current status. What you have always done is comforting and predictable. Change requires courage and possibly more initial loneliness as a result of the people witnessing the shift in your life. You must start with freeing yourself from the early seeded idea of struggle.

THERE ARE THREE STEPS TO STRUGGLE FREEDOM

1. People who want something are ready to look within and ask questions. Questions like, "Why isn't this happening for me?" You will be ready to have a true heart to healing conversation with yourself. You may seek a

coach or therapist to help you explore your 'Why?' You will be able to accept a loving awareness of yourself. You will be able to hold yourself accountable for your own happiness. It takes raw realness at this point.

2. If someone is determined to create a change she will learn. She will explore and discern all that she needs. Of course, this is a commitment of time, emotional resources. and possibly money. She will gladly invest in herself. She will have no issue investing in herself because she has unconditional love and sees her value. People spend money on things they find valuable. She will ask questions, read books, seek consultation and carefully observe and stay mindful about her life.

   If your friend is not taking these steps, she is lying. which brings us to the last step.

3. Stop lying! In my therapist days, I became aware of this lying epidemic. Now to be fair, there may be other words to describe this phenomenon such as subconscious awareness or denial. Whether intentional or unintentional, a lie means you are not sitting in truth. Some truths are blinded by emotion or the story that someone told you. It is often the therapist's job to confront and challenge 'the lie'. The lies may be self-destructive or protective. No matter the purpose, the lie keeps you from the truth.

   You may be wondering how to know what a lie is.

Easy! I look for what doesn't match. Things that align stay together. For example, a person who truly values herself and practices awareness will not have relationships that are full of shallow, abusive, and dishonest companions. It just doesn't align. It doesn't make sense. Which sends a message that one of these things is not true. It's not enough to just think positively; struggle is an energy that attracts.

I DON'T HAVE TO FIGHT

I repeatedly attracted unhealthy relationships with emotionally traumatized people. Were there really that many emotionally traumatized people? I don't believe so, but I attracted all the traumatized people. Unconsciously, I was a magnet. There were emotionally responsive people available, but I was addicted to struggle. Being in healthy relationships means looking within, learning how to be different, seeking help, and the most important part, I had to stop lying to myself.

Not lying to myself has been one of the hardest tasks ever. I minimized cruel behavior with the story I would tell myself. I didn't have to spend too much time in hurt feelings because I minimized the damage. I also reinforced and gave permission for torment. It's a destructive cycle and hopefully you see the need for self-compassion.

Relationships even the painful ones take work to sort through. You have to conduct an emotional autopsy and find the cause of this pain. Coming to the truth is an awakening process. One must give up the go-to excuses, denial, and minimizing. I was so addicted to struggle I never felt like I could let it go. What would I do without the struggle?

The answer is often simple. If something that you want isn't showing up for you, go through the steps to struggle freedom. You will be able to figure out why. You won't have a long monologue filled with everyone who let you down. You won't center it around your perceived superficial shortcomings. You will know your truth!

Your truth may sound like;
I am afraid of this happening,
I self-sabotage,
I don't think I am worthy,
I haven't figured out how to love myself.

The truth is simple, and the answer is always simple. When we are ready to stop fighting and give up the struggle, we are ready to receive the gifts of compassion and then clarity.

END THE STRUGGLE GET REAL

R.E.A.L- RADICAL EMPATHIC ACCEPTANCE OF LIFE

real

ADJECTIVE

1. actually existing as a thing or occurring in fact; not imagined or supposed.

RADICAL

Throughout this book is an accounting of my *real* life. It's not everything, but it's a journey of a life full of chaos, confusion, disappointment, grace, and compassion. It is not imagined.

Any of my life challenges would have justified staying 'in the box' of limitations. Poverty could have stolen my hope of stability and reproduced generations of poverty. My broken relationships could have left me guarded and insecure. Having a mother unable to provide validation and nurturing created grief so great I didn't think anything could heal it.

Your pain may be like mine and even differ in magnitude. One guarantee is the radical shift that occurred in my faith. My faith began to challenge my past. I began to think about what I needed to be different in my life. It took decades to form the patterns of thoughts and behavior that became familiar. Changing the negative cycles that hurt and keep us from our greatest selves is radical. It is radical to even consider that this pattern could change.

So much of our energy is devoted to hiding and minimizing our trauma and fears, it is radical to sit with those emotions. It's radical to accept what happened without excuses or positive illusions. The shame of the little girl with food stamps returns whenever money fears arise. It is radical to create a story that didn't end with being a victim of bad men. When I stopped hoping that the last time I forgave my mom would be the last time that was radical. The truth is radical. Sitting in your skin and being content in a world seeking constant attention and validation is radical.

Often being radical is seen as being a leader to thousands of people versus growing in your own self-awareness. A radical life is not a war; it is complex and ever evolving. Have you fully recognized yourself? Have you told yourself the truth about you and allowed it to exist alongside all that you hope for in life? I stopped being resistant. I stopped running from the sad parts of myself. Connecting with all of me is radical.

EMPATHIC

Connecting with radical truth opens the door to empathy. All my life being sensitive to energy and spirit meant one thing. It meant I was going to have to lie about what I was feeling. It meant blocking what I felt because I couldn't explain it in words. We all have intuition and I learned to shut my intuition off for fear nobody would understand. I wanted to be so careful and to protect against the judgement of the people around me. In many ways, my empathy was a gift.

Dr. Ramini Durvasula talks about empathy being a magnet for narcissists. I am a survivor of narcissist and borderline injuries.

My valuable gift of empathy allows me to show up with understanding and compassion. I wanted to run out and heal people. I wanted to save them from the next terrible decision. I am convinced that my level of empathy was attracting emotionally needy people.

Then one day I realized, nobody was being fixed. I devoted a lot of time but people were more committed to the comfort of themselves than the challenges of change. Change was difficult and slow moving. I changed my approach from giving advice to listening with compassion.

I heard what was being said and what was not. When things didn't change fast enough, most people gave up. Soon I acknowledged that my empathy was misdirected. I was spending so much time trying to understand other people's processes and feelings that I neglected to show empathy for myself. The understanding of my own feelings were missing.

I ran to this brokenness and sat in it for a while, trying to understand how all of this happened and what happened to my family, my relationships, and myself. I knew I made progress when I found happiness with the truth.

For so long, sharing my own feelings brought up so many fears in other people. A therapist has to know how to hold space for people without being afraid to go where is needed. You also have to hold space for yourself and those parts that are still healing. Some people were so committed to not questioning anything. My feelings were suppressed so long, it was a process to find my feelings again. I had to learn how to express my feelings without apology. I began this journey with a radical shift in thinking and moved toward a great deal of empathy. Both empathy for myself and compassion for those that hurt me could live together at the same time.

ACCEPTANCE

Accepting that you can't change the past may be the most challenging stage of life. People in therapy are there because of what happened to them in the past. The past is so powerful that many of us use it to fear the future. I learned this very special mantra about acceptance and letting go.

I release you and set you free from my thinking, speaking, and anything I once desired

Anytime I am stuck wanting to change the past I meditate on this statement. There are times you get stuck in your past and sometimes you get stuck in someone else's story. We are watching their lives like a movie. We see the bad guy in the shadow before them. We want them to run. We want them to take the other path. Letting go means creating an unconditional love not based on someone accepting our guidance.

We live our lives with the acceptance that we are responsible for our own happiness. People may join us in life and teach us more about ourselves. I began to accept that we are all seeking compassion for our imperfections. We have a universal need to feel heard and connected to others. Most of what we do, whether right or wrong, is an effort to find an attachment. We all want a soft place to fall. Acceptance may take time therapy, coaching, and deep reflection.

OF LIFE

Life is challenging, and at times, confusing. There is so much in life that remains out of our control. When you think about the great impact of Dr. Martin Luther King Jr, you know one life can touch so many. His life was purposefully driven. We can choose to change the world with a powerful movement. His life was a great example of being radical and empathic. We get to decide every day how we want to impact the world. Life is about affirmations and surrender. We are powerful and recognizing our gifts despite our adversity inspires everyone around us. My purpose was saving people from my experience and in that, I learned that I had to save myself. I save myself with awareness, compassion, and intention every single day.

Conclusion

Don't let your experience dictate what you're allowed to hope for.

Even when life is not all figured out, it's part of our story. Loss is a gift that offers deeper awareness. When I depended on others for my needs that awareness diminished. There has been a lot of loss. The only consistency in my life is loss. I almost lost a whole family through trauma, drugs, mental illness, shame, and resentment.

Through all the loss I became obsessed with things being predictable. I thought if things were predictable and never changed, they would always be there. I could depend on it. My thinking defied the natural order of life. Everything will change. How was I supposed to grow and not change? I got attached to the idea of people never changing and sought after the unchanging things. This made life hard. I feared change yet wanted to grow. I had to embrace them both. Unpredictable growth and change created humility and compassion

I am giving myself what I need. I am asking for support and challenging the idea I have to do it all by myself. Affirmations, prayers, and mindfulness joined my journey. I have surrendered hope that I could change anything in the past. I am forgiving the inability of those who were not able to love me due to their own brokenness.

God knows it wasn't easy or quick. When you've felt defeated so long, giving up seems irresistible. It wasn't simply will power and making better choices. People and things had to be removed. People focus so much on the will power to say no rather than creating an optimal environment for a healthy life. You are going to have to remove access. Suppose we were surrounded by only great options. There is no decision that is difficult when any option would be a good choice. The decision is half the battle. Fill your life with wonderful options. If you hold on to the struggle and hide it in that back closet, you will grab it whenever doubt creeps in. You will pull it out when shame arrives. Figure out the struggle and its deeper meaning so you can get REAL.

I decided to have a better life and sought after what that meant for me. My loss created a desire for a family full of love and creativity. My family isn't perfect just healthier. My family is whoever I choose, not limited to blood relatives. I am grateful I had my son. His need to live a good life didn't leave me much time to feel pitiful. If I wanted to be on this life journey with him, I had to live a great life as well. He was the foundation of love that made me want to even think about changing my life.

My child's life was not going to be a series of sad events living in trauma ordained by chaos and limited by fear. If I didn't have him, I don't know if I would have changed anything. I am just now realizing the hope our relationship gives to so many. People thought I was brave to go back to grad school with a 6-month old baby. At the same time, I was full of fear and felt I was out of options. I didn't feel brave at all.

I was courageous to people even when I didn't feel brave at all. I don't want to make it seem like love was all I needed but it was all I needed. Love was tremendous, I saw the world through his eyes. Accompanying him through his childhood offered me so much insight and healing. When I became Zuri's mom I had never worked a full-time job, I wasn't accustomed to a year-round steady paycheck but now the idea of not having one was uncomfortable. I lived off loans, worked weekends, lived in Section 8 housing and applied for food stamps. I didn't want to live off $26,000 a year, so grad school was a great option. My child's life wasn't going to struggle. I decided that he was not going to struggle like I did, that was courageous.

Thichnanhan says, without suffering you have no ways to learn to be u nderstanding and compassionate. The gift of compassion is tremendous.

THE END

References

5 Reasons Why Social Workers Need to Be Rich. (2015, January 19). Retrieved from https://www.huffingtonpost.com/eva-forde/5-reasons-why-social-work_b_6187678

Ford, T. (2019, September 11). Brene Brown Net Worth 2018: Wiki, Married, Family, Wedding, Salary, Siblings. Retrieved from https://networthpost.com/brene-brown-net-worth

The Fresh Air Fund fact sheet 2019. (n.d.). Retrieved from freshair.org

What is Section 8? (n.d.). Retrieved from https://affordablehousingonline.com/housing-help/What-Is-Section-8

Author's Biography

Khadijah Tishan Washington MSW, LCSW was born in Harlem, New York. She credits her own creative and chaotic childhood with inspiring her passion of social work. Khadijah began her journey of service and self- healing in child and family mental health. As a Licensed Clinical Social Worker, she serves as the mentoring chair for the National Association of Black Social Workers- Richmond Chapter as well as the chair of the Social Work Advisory Committee at Virginia Union University. She hosts the Money, Men & Mentals podcast offering R.E.A.L. (Radical Empathic Acceptance of Life) tools for people from challenging backgrounds to show up to their lives more abundantly.

Made in the USA
Middletown, DE
02 July 2021